Norman Foster

Daniel Treiber

E & FN SPON
An Imprint of Chapman & Hall

London · Glasgow · Weinheim · New York · Tokyo · Melbourne · Madras

Published by E & FN Spon, an imprint of Chapman & Hall, 2–6 Boundary Row, London SE1 8HN, UK

Chapman & Hall, 2–6 Boundary Row, London SE1 8HN, UK

Blackie Academic and Professional, Wester Cleddens Road, Bishopbriggs, Glasgow G64 2NZ, UK

Chapman & Hall GmbH, Pappelallee 3, 69469 Weinheim, Germany

Chapman & Hall USA, 115 Fifth Avenue, New York, NY 10003, USA

Chapman & Hall Japan, ITP-Japan, Kyowa Building, 3F, 2-2-1 Hirakawacho, Chiyoda-ku, Tokyo 102, Japan

Chapman & Hall Australia, 102 Dodds Street, South Melbourne, Victoria 3205, Australia

Chapman & Hall India, R. Seshadri, 32 Second Main Road, CIT East, Madras 600 035, India

English language edition 1995

© 1995 E & FN Spon

Original German language edition *Norman Foster*, © 1992, Birkhäuser Verlag AG, Basel/Switzerland

Translated by Christian Caryl

Typeset in 11/12.3pt Rockwell by Photoprint, Torquay, Devon
Printed in Hong Kong

ISBN 0 419 20320 6

A catalogue record for this book is available from the British Library

Library of Congress Catalog Card Number: 95-68510

Norman Foster

LEEDS COLLEGE OF ART AND DESIGN

JK

■ Architecture
Collection

Contents

Charles and Ray Eames,
Eames House (Case
Study House No. 8) in
Pacific Palisades,
California, 1945–49.

America

The house stands at the end of a boulevard lined by eucalyptus trees; behind it, far below, is the ocean. Seen from the side, its dark outline is reminiscent of a traditional Japanese house – despite the diagonal wind bracing and the red-blue-yellow-white opaque panels on the façade, which recall a Mondrian painting. The original intention of its creator, the designer and architect Charles Eames, was that the house would be raised on a substructure so that its residents could enjoy the panoramic view of the ocean. But when the construction elements were delivered, he became intrigued by the idea of putting them to better use and creating the most spacious building possible. He came up with a new design in which these steel components were used to the very last piece. Instead of being designed on the drawing board, the structural elements were selected, in pre-fabricated form, from a catalogue. This self-imposed limitation of standardized components produced, as a consequence, a bold composition of smooth surfaces; the simplicity of the plain components, and their completely natural combination gave the Eames House a freshness and liveliness that it has preserved to the present day. Not least due to the way it was created, the house occupies a special place in the history of architectural design.

At the beginning of the 1960s, two young English architects named Richard Rogers and Norman Foster, both freshly graduated from architecture school, paid a visit to the Eames House. It was part of the 'Case Study Houses' programme sponsored by the California architecture magazine *Arts and Architecture* and its editor John Entenza. The six model homes created after the Eames House of 1949 by Pierre Koenig, Craig Ellwood and Raphael Soriano are all expressions of the same idea: to apply the modular grid associated with steel structures, with the aim of achieving industrialized construction. Here as in their later works the architects regarded lightness as the basis for all their designs, and in fact most of the buildings used steel columns and beams with small cross-sections in narrow-span grids.[1] Structural considerations are naturally fundamental in the construction of a house; in all these houses of the 1950s, however, the grid and the three-dimensional lattice play a key role in their formal, spatial, and logical construction. They may owe this to the teachings of one of the masters of modern architecture, Ludwig Mies van der Rohe. Yet their light, lean profiles place the houses of the Californian avant-garde in stark contrast to the monumentality of structure demanded by Mies. They are completely free of that 'heroism' of European style, which grows out of the avant-garde mentality and the bathos of a new order.

The Eames House presents an admirable impression of fragility and physical lightness, but also of heart. These houses are free from all

[1] The terraced roof, this insignia of modern architecture since the 1920s, was refined by opening up its structure to the inside, thus producing a visual contrast to the columns and cladding.

Pierre Koenig, Steel house (Case Study House No. 22) in Los Angeles, California, 1959–60. Pierre Koenig, single-family house (Case Study House No. 21) near Hollywood, California, 1958.

that is tragic, as if the architects succeeded in simultaneously over-coming the weight of the structure and the fate of the avant-garde artists. These relaxed, almost impersonal pavilions of steel present a new view of the modern spirit in architecture: formal neutrality; minimalism; industrially manufactured materials; regular, at times rigidly symmetrical floor plans; but also simple, direct flexibility within the grid plan, which is actually rigid only in appearance. This is an architecture without oppressiveness, without preconditions or con-ventions, which would go on to leave its mark on the era.

THE AMERICAN SCENE AROUND 1960

The two young architects who visited the Eames House in 1962 met at Yale University in New Haven, Connecticut. Norman Foster, from a working class family in northern England, had already completed his studies in Manchester. There he had learned how to produce schemes to deadlines, how to detail a structure, how to ensure coordination and consistency of the drawings in a project. Richard Rogers, in turn, came from the Architectural Association, where he had received a completely different education that fostered his enjoyment of discussion and his intellectual curiosity without, however, teaching him draughting skills or planning discipline. His family was scattered around the world and had strong connections with Italy, where his uncle, the architect Ernesto Rogers, was invigor-ating the architectural debate of those years. As Yale students in the studio of Paul Rudolph, a well-known personality at the time, Foster and Rogers often worked together. They discovered that they were personally compatible and their work was complementary: Rogers's elegant ideas were difficult to represent, Foster's graceful sketches brilliantly brought them to life.[2]

At this time American architecture was in upheaval. While the famous architects of the 1950s happily adopted the slogans of the great creators of modernity, such as Walter Gropius or Mies van der Rohe, by 1960 a younger generation was freeing itself from the masters.[3] But even more important was that architects such as Louis Kahn or Eero Saarinen were questioning the most basic laws of modern architec-ture. Saarinen, who died in 1961, openly transcended them in order to work out a specific style for each commission, always with the same force and the same abundance of imagination. His most important works give an impression of immediacy, achieving a synthesis of plastic effect and definite structure. At the beginning of the 1950s, Louis Kahn generated considerable attention with his building for the art gallery at Yale University; when Rogers and Foster were at Yale, Kahn had just completed the Richards Medical Research Building in Philadelphia and had worked on the laboratory buildings for the Salk

[2] Cf. Bryan Appleyard, *Richard Rogers – A Biography*, Faber and Faber, 1986, p. 97.

[3] This is demonstrated, for example, by the buildings of Philip Johnson: his 1956 synagogue in Port Chester and his 1959 Asia House in New York show few traces of his great model Mies van der Rohe.

Institute in San Diego. Both schemes continue the development of an idea that served as the basis for his Trenton Bath House of 1954–59. It is a small building, but designed according to a formal principal which follows its own logic and an abstract geometry at the same time – a simple figure, axially structured, with a distinction between 'servant and served rooms' that stands in contrast to the *plan libre* so valued by Mies and Le Corbusier. On the one hand the architectural expression is simplified, on the other the hierarchies have increased in importance.

Thus America greatly enriched Foster; it was there that he met his future partner, whose background and education differed from his own, but who complemented and stimulated him – an incentive that challenged him to outdo the other, to outdo himself. He also met James Stirling, who taught at Yale for a short time and whose acquaintance would also prove useful later on. He discovered American modernism – contemporary modernism as well as the masters Wright and Mies, whose work he saw in Chicago. He absorbed these various aspects of contemporary architecture, all these different, often opposing formal or conceptual approaches. For Foster America also brought the discovery of a new sense of scale, a spaciousness just as suited to the landscape as to the mentality of its inhabitants, who were capable of enthusiasm, who believed in innovations and placed their trust in youth, whilst old Europe remained slightly cold and reserved.

THE BRITISH SCENE AROUND 1960

England had turned to modern architecture after the war amid the enthusiasm of reconstruction. Yet that which the British regarded as modern was actually a rather moderate variant, generally known in Great Britain as 'the Swedish Style'. In contrast to the increasing roughness of the avant-garde, the *béton brut* praised by Le Corbusier and the steel of Mies van der Rohe, Scandinavian architecture offered the British public a gentler alternative. But it was not the work of the great Finn, Alvar Aalto, or the elegant creations of Gunnar Asplund that received the most positive reception, rather the tamer and less sophisticated forms of contemporary Swedish and Danish architecture. Britons sought 'comfortable simplicity', the free use of 'natural materials', a 'close connection with the surrounding landscape' – in short, a respectable modernism whose principal archetypes can be seen in Arne Jacobsen's maisonettes in Soeholm-Klampenbord (1950): comfortable modernism with a slanting roof.[4]

The other face shown to the British public by modern architecture was the Royal Festival Hall of 1951. The Festival of Britain was planned for the centenary of the Great Exhibition of 1851 that provided the

[4] The more austere features of Jacobsen's architecture were ignored. His school in Gentofte (1952–56) anticipates, to a certain degree, Rogers's and Foster's search for structures of maximum simplicity in its principle of the regular grid.

James Stirling,
residential buildings in
Ham Common,
Richmond, London,
1957.

world with a cult building for generations of architects: the Crystal Palace. The Royal Festival Hall evolved from a group of more or less imaginative temporary buildings, and it was the first public building in which the modern style finally established itself in Great Britain. Though it had a lasting effect on public opinion, it presented a somewhat more picturesque image that was far removed from the actual rationalist aspirations of the Modern Movement.

In the years to come students found examples in the architects who decisively resisted such gentle modernisms, such as Peter and Alison Smithson and James Stirling. Two projects by the Smithsons attracted particular attention: the expansion of the University of Sheffield (1953) and the Hunstanton School (1954). The competition entry for Sheffield, an 'anti-art' version of brutalism, appears intentionally hard, 'sado-masochistic', to quote the English critic Colin Rowe. The Hunstanton School is less harsh but displays the same striving toward clarity: the building is conventionally rectangular, reflecting the Smithsons' rejection of a picturesque compromise along the lines of Festival Hall, and it has nothing of the aesthetic refinement of a Mies. The building's services are unashamedly exposed and the construction is simple and honest, with no sculptural handling of the surface. Despite a strong graphic effect it is the rough and the hard that predominate. There is a distinct contrast in the work of the second architect, who became successful in England at the same time, James Stirling. When his building at Leicester University in 1963 gained him an international reputation, he had already attracted attention with his design of the apartments in Ham Common between 1955 and 1958. The influence of the Jaoul Houses of Le Corbusier is immediately apparent. Like the Smithsons, Stirling attempts to take the path of modernism without imitating the masters. His buildings are challenging in their unorthodoxy, but they are of superior quality, harmonious in scale, and filled with refinements that deserve to be enjoyed. They attest to his sense of the aesthetic and to a standard of drawing that we will encounter again in the work of Foster.

Foster completed his studies in Manchester with the conviction, which was shared by Rogers and many other young architects, that the new architecture was borne by moral sincerity. Here, incidentally, he followed the call of Stirling, who, whether he wanted to or not, played the role of the grand old man for many. But the end of CIAM in 1957 had drastic effects on the British scene: the direct questioning of the principles established by the masters left the debate unresolved; there was no clear directive, no ideological basis that could have supported a doctrine. It was left to each individual to set his own rules, to select his models, to define his modernity.

TEAM 4

When Norman Foster returned to London in 1963, he found himself hired by Rogers for a practice to be called 'Team 4'. The group included Georgie Cheesman, Richard's former fiancée, and her sister Wendy. Several days after a copper plate with the name of the team had been mounted on the building, Georgie resigned from the group. This posed a problem, for at the time she was the only one who possessed the right to submit plans: in England the architect's diploma is insufficient by itself, one must be registered by the Architects' Registration Council. At first there were also other difficulties: Norman was very reserved toward Wendy, this exceptional woman who seemed the virtual opposite of his creativity. Their relationship relaxed only once it had developed into a love affair. They married in 1964 and had two children. Marcus Brumwell, whose daughter Su[5] was married to Rogers, became Team 4's first client. Brumwell, the very successful director of an advertising agency, had been intensely interested in contemporary art ever since meeting the great painter Ben Nicholson before the war; henceforth he would also be linked with Nicholson by an anti-fascist attitude in their politics. Nicholson had introduced him to modernism, creating an inclination that would later lead him to become president of the Arts and Science Committee in the Labour Party. As a family member Brumwell was also sympathetic to Rogers' and Foster's artistic ambitions and tolerant of their lack of professional experience; moreover he was sufficiently non-conformist to make a reality of an out-of-the-ordinary project.

[5] Su Brumwell had joined the team after Georgie Cheeseman's departure.

THE COCKPIT AND CREEK VEAN

The first commission from the Brumwells was a small shelter – an all-weather gazebo – to be used during the period of the conversion of their existing house in Cornwall. The 'Cockpit' is located on a promontory that juts into the Fal estuary. One cannot imagine a smaller commission, and yet Team 4 produced a sensible and clearly formed architectural solution. It combines an almost animalistic adaptation to the surrounding woodland with a very efficient and yet poetic command of architectural forms and materials. An angular base embedded in the ground supports a glass canopy, facing the sea, whose tent-like form integrates itself into the undulating floor of the forest.

Hiring an engineer had originally been considered unnecessary, but the young architects chose to obtain the advice of Tony Hunt, whom they had met shortly before.[6] Hunt worked on both the Cockpit and the house itself. He declared emphatically that the intended conversion of the Victorian building would be significantly more expensive than a completely new building. Brumwell agreed to a new building, and Team 4 then proposed roughly 50 variants until a

[6] Hunt had worked primarily for Samuely, ran his own practice, and was already experienced in collaboration with somewhat eccentric architects.

Norman Foster, work
from his student
period. Below: Rufford
Hall, Cheshire, July
1959. Detail sketches of
the timber connections
(oak) in the roof.

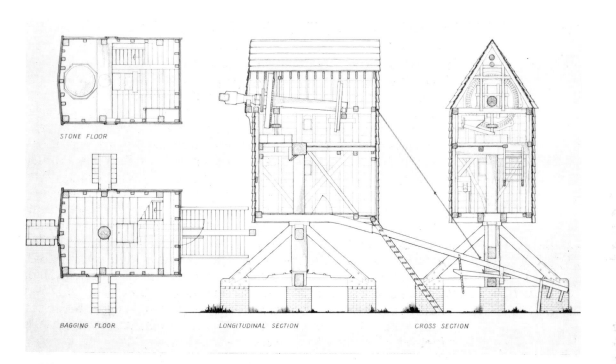

STONE FLOOR

BAGGING FLOOR

LONGITUDINAL SECTION

CROSS SECTION

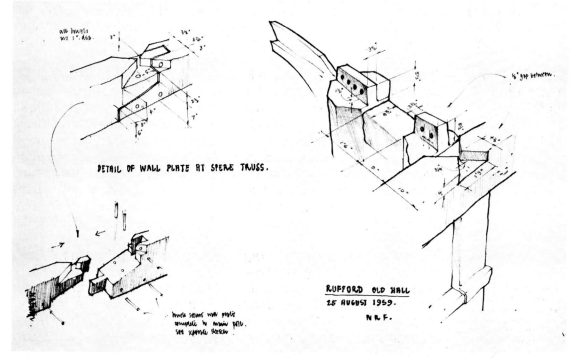

DETAIL OF WALL PLATE AT SPERE TRUSS.

RUFFORD OLD HALL
25 AUGUST 1959.
N.R.F.

Team 4, the Retreat
('Cockpit') at Pill Creek,
Feock, Cornwall, 1964.

scheme was finally approved. Its details underwent modification even as it was being built.

An early scheme for Creek Vean incorporated three stacked floors, stepped back to follow the slope of the terrain, under a large raking window wall. It was abandoned in favour of two clearly separated volumes between which a large open stairway led down the slope. The house is designed along two axes, which Foster called 'routes'. One, the outer route, is connected with the access road above the house by a path and leads down to an old boathouse on the shore. The other route, more a *promenade architecturale*, connects all the internal rooms, from the terraced roof down to the entrance of an underground garage. The alignment of the rooms follows the contour of the site; a sliding door allows the rooms to be opened onto the most important element of the internal axis, the gallery housing the picture collection. This gallery lies, as if in a crevice, between the slope and the living rooms. During the day it receives light through a slanted glass roof,[7] at night it is lit by outdoor spotlights in the style of Aalto.

Viewed from the road, the formal treatment of the walls recalls the Californian buildings of Frank Lloyd Wright.[8] The graphic geometry of the floor plan, which is at once free and angular, also alludes to Wright's later work, with its fan-like arrangement and with the great austerity of parallel lines, the preference for sharp angles and the angular stairways as if cut from a crystal. But any direct references are carefully avoided: the floor plan favoured by Wright, with its crossed axes, has been transformed into overlapping paths, similar to Le Corbusier's idea of a *promenade architecturale*. Even if the geometry of the floor plan is influenced by Wright, any risk of epigonal imitation is skilfully avoided with the cubic volumes, the grassed terrace roofs, and the slate floors – this also a reference to Le Corbusier. In admirable fashion the architects maintain their distance from the great masters, the fashionable new stars and conventional English architecture. Foster and Rogers may adopt ideas, strategies and formal methods, but all is carefully re-thought and re-interpreted.[9] The house, completed in 1964, met with great acclaim in architectural circles. In 1969 it received an RIBA award, the first family home to do so. Foster and Rogers, nurtured by their client, could thus begin their careers in a very un-British way: a young American, Japanese or Swiss architect can establish 'his work' with a spectacular building, but rarely a British architect.

[7] The neoprene seals used for the glass roof were an innovation at the time; Roche and Dinkeloo, the former assistants of Saarinen, had worked with them before.

[8] One need only compare the honey colour of the walls and the structural complexity of its 'folds'.

[9] The 'trademark' of the masters, such as Mies's steel cubes, Le Corbusier's *pilotis*, and Wright's roof shapes, are not adopted here, tellingly enough.

THE JAFFÉ
HOUSE AND
MURRAY MEWS

The house for Michael Jaffé attracted less attention even though it marks a significant turning point. Though its relationship to the ground remains important, now Wrightian romanticism makes room for a

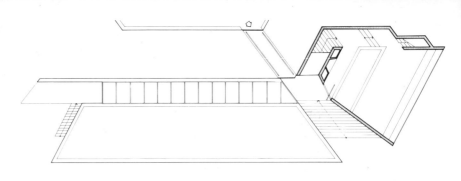

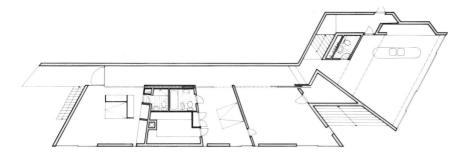

Team 4, Creek Vean at Pill Creek, Feock, Cornwall, 1964. View from above and inside the gallery.

rational geometry that found the approbation of James Stirling. The house, christened 'Skybreak' by Foster, takes its strict division between served and servant rooms from Kahn and its sense of space from Stirling. The principal view is to the north, the road lies to the south. For this reason large slanting glass walls and roofs provide light to the interior of the house. The influx of light from above is not accented as dramatically as is generally the case with Wright and Le Corbusier; the effect is more domestic, despite the modernity of the architectural handwriting. The solution appears as a preliminary stage, for here is a taste of the future big projects: in the treatment of light, in the depth of the floor plan and its flexibility, which is provided here by sliding walls between central zones of the house.

The three houses of Murray Mews, their radical design equally influenced by Stirling, once again take up the idea of the Cockpit: a massive base construction receives light through a large glass roof. But it was above all the bad experiences that would remain for the architects. Work on site with a less tolerant client and an apparently unscrupulous contractor was extremely difficult. The most remarkable anecdote tells of damp-proof membranes that were, in fact, newspaper painted black.[10] These experiences, as well as the fact that the architects' working drawings, in which they had invested a great deal of time, were ignored, confirmed Rogers and Foster in their negative view of traditional construction companies, the so-called 'wet trades'.[11]

Team 4 also worked extensively with the planning of small groups of single-family houses. The most representative of these projects was situated opposite Creek Vean, on the other side of the estuary 'Waterfront Housing'. These were not to be typical suburban houses; instead, the style refers strongly to local vernacular architecture and blends with the landscape as harmoniously as Creek Vean does. The houses, integrated into the slope and stepped on several levels, were angled so that their sides faced the sea and the south. Brumwell had acquired the site, but a poll of local residents revealed resistance to the scheme and planning permission was not granted. The other projects for groups of houses were likewise never built.

[10] Cf. Bryan Appleyard, *Richard Rogers – A Biography*, Faber and Faber, 1986, p. 113.

[11] The name alludes to the use of water during construction.

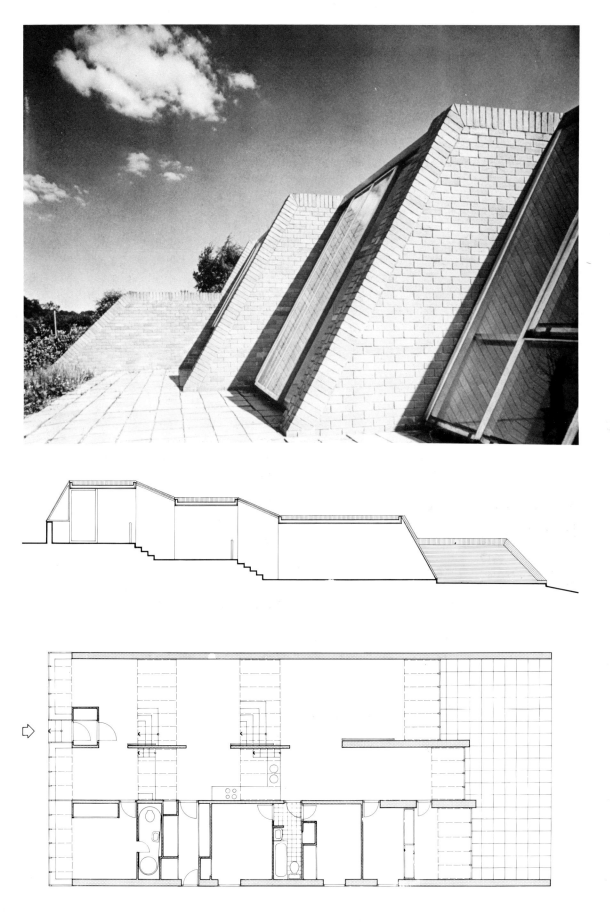

Buildings for industry

It was thanks to the mediation of James Stirling that Rogers and Foster received their first commission from industry. Stirling, asked for recommendations by the owner of the British company Reliance Controls, had suggested three teams of architects. The brief was to construct within ten months (including design) an industrial building of rather modest dimensions, which would, however, easily allow extension to three times its size.

With this building of 1965 Foster and Rogers developed many of the characteristics that would henceforth distinguish their style; most importantly, they discovered their preferred material, steel. Though the Smithsons' Hunstanton School building was unquestionably one of the models for the design, the two young architects owed much more to the California School. The knowledge of industrial processes and products had already enabled Charles Eames and his compatriots to design their experimental buildings with industrial components and to create buildings of great flexibility. That the factory for Reliance Controls had to be built in an extremely short period also made the use of pre-fabricated standard elements much more appealing than the building method – conventional, tedious and prone to many setbacks – that Rogers and Foster had employed for their first buildings. Transforming the traditional construction site, with all its unpredictabilities and irritating delays, into an assembly site for pre-fabricated construction elements promised considerable savings in time and encouraged hopes for better implementation, fewer unpleasant surprises, and greater reliability. Use of steel structure and cladding was dictated by necessity. But as Foster and Rogers, assisted by Tony Hunt, approached the very limits of the performance of the material, new paths began to open up. Striving toward the smallest possible cross-sections, they realized that steel was a virtually unexplored realm for architecture. The architectural success of Reliance Controls[12] is due to the extraordinary freedom that the two architects created for themselves within the technical parameters of the project.

The building is characterized by a clear sense of horizontality, emphasized by a large elevated water tank reminiscent of the Hunstanton School. The treatment of the detailing goes well beyond pure functionality.[13] Unlike the Smithsons' school, the corners appear almost sculptural. As with Mies, the façade is defined by its architectural organization, despite a certain Californian casualness in comparison with the neo-classical model. It is distinguished by elegance and imagination and the relationship between the structural elements, as well as between structure and cladding, is clearly visible. As with Mies the floor plan is of absolute simplicity; it radicalizes the Californian experiments of the Case Study Houses and makes them, in retrospect, appear almost picturesque.

[12] Cf. Bryan Appleyard, *Richard Rogers – A Biography*, Faber and Faber, 1986, p. 129.

[13] For example, Hunt recalls that they finally came to a decision to increase the bracing joints, a central detail, only after long hesitation and at the very last minute.

After the difficulties with the previous buildings, the structural and aesthetic success of steel here was a revelation. On this basis the two architects developed a design vocabulary of unusual austerity. Rogers viewed the incorporation of building services into the structure as increasingly problematic, and he began to move toward a more supple style. For Foster, in contrast, the aim of perfect integration of the various components became a veritable obsession.[14] The expansion of the repertoire brought with it a typological renewal of the corporate building. The simplicity of the quadratic plan, which combines production areas and offices, allows complete equality within the building's structural organization: no separation between 'white collar' and 'blue collar' employees, no hierarchy between the areas of the building, a single entrance, a common canteen. This approach demanded a re-orientation of the design process, which now had to be supported by intensive persuasion of the clients. After Reliance Controls, dialogue and consultation grew steadily in importance for Foster – with consultants, but also with owners, decision-makers and employees as the future users.

[14] "Roof and floor represent the well-thought-out attempt to bring structure and building services into close connection with the profiles and cladding of the rooftop installations, which function in turn as reflectors for the neon strips. The Reliance Works was a turning point in our attempt to unify social, technical, and operational requirements" (Norman Foster, Lecture before the RIBA [Royal Institute of British Architects]), June 21, 1983.

THE END OF TEAM 4

Although the Reliance Controls factory won a prize from *Architectural Design*[15] magazine in 1966, new commissions failed to materialize. The mood in Team 4 had changed. Now it consisted of two married couples, which inevitably led to friction. In June 1967 Rogers and Foster decided to close down their joint office. Richard and Su worked together until 1971, when their success in the competition for the Pompidou Centre necessitated the establishment of a collaboration between Rogers and Piano. Norman and Wendy established Foster Associates in 1967.

[15] For the *Financial Times* it was 'the most remarkable industrial building' of 1967.

Amid an intense and stimulating climate of competition, Rogers and Foster had taken just a few years – applying all their strength out of love of their work – to create a remarkable style. They demonstrated an ability to make use of the simplest things, to develop consistently elementary structures and to imbue them with a surprising presence. Despite all their radicalism they were also capable of bringing strong ideas to completion without fundamental concessions.

While Rogers, in the years to come, would develop steel buildings completely different from the previous works, realizing new ideas again and again, Foster explored the realms of industry and business. With a few exceptions[16] he would spend the next decade concentrating on the design of workplaces. Stylistically Foster now approached Saarinen and his pupils (Daniel, Mann, Johnson and Mendenhall in Los Angeles and Cesar Pelli) by concealing the structure behind a reflecting skin stretched like a soap bubble, freed from all that is

[16] Exceptions are the housing development in Milton Keynes and the Palmerston School, both from 1975.

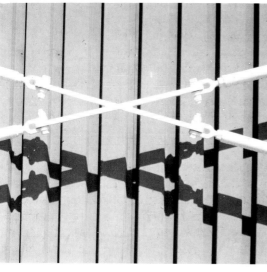

IBM Cosham, Hampshire,
1970–71.

[17] The 1968 project for an inflatable office for Computer Technology Ltd. takes the idea of the membrane as an external skin to an extreme: walls and roof are formed by a nylon-reinforced PVC fabric.

metallic, up the entire height of the building.[17] His formal ambitions, in their modernism characteristic of the projects from the period between 1968 and 1975, ultimately give way to a functional concept more strongly influenced by the site and brief for each project. It was this problem that would henceforth determine the selection of architectural approach. Several clients enabled the architect to bring social, technical and commercial concerns into harmony: Fred Olsen, Computer Technology Limited and IBM.

MODERN OFFICE CONSTRUCTION

Several projects were completed for the Fred Olsen shipping line. As well as schemes for Vestby and Oslo that were never built, Foster designed the administrative headquarters and passenger terminal in London. The significance of this relatively small commission lies in its precise response to needs: Foster's critical analysis of his client's ideas about the character and site of the building led to a dialogue with management and the union that actually gave birth to the project. The completed building even transformed the attitudes of the employees. Previously in disrepute because of their coarse behaviour, they were now concerned to protect the building by forbidding passing truck drivers to use it 'because of their bad habits'![18]

[18] Foster reported this in his 1983 lecture before the RIBA.

The Newport School project marks another decisive step in the design of compact buildings: all zones of activity are unified under a single roof for better exploitation of the site, as well as for an improvement in social interaction. The façade stands in the tradition of the Eames House[19] and the Californian modernism of Craig Ellwood. Though the project was not built, it served as invaluable experience for the first commission of IBM in Cosham.

[19] A component system was created from already available standard elements; the lightweight structure was designed to provide great flexibility for the various methods of teaching and to combine all installations as if under an umbrella.

The individual building solution worked out for IBM enabled the preservation of all trees on the site, thus creating the impression of a park on the edge of the city. The equally simple and impressive façades of the long building consist of reflective glass panels that extend the full height and are connected by neoprene joints. The structure and roof are slightly set back. The building's inherent flexibility enabled continued changes in the mix of activities: working practices were altered and the users were able to introduce new systems for security, telecommunications and data processing.

Businessmen were beginning to recognize that the development of their activities is difficult to forecast and that buildings and facilities thus require flexibility both in size and structure. The result was the development of a type of industrial building that permitted frequent and extensive restructuring of internal spaces. Flexibility in this sense

Flexible hall
constructions: Wiltshire
School, Newport, Gwent,
1967 competition entry,
not built. Palmerston
Special School, Liverpool,
1974–75. Administrative
and recreation centre for
the Fred Olsen Ltd.
shipping line, Millwall
Docks, London, 1968–69.

Modern workplaces:
Factory for Reliance
Controls Ltd., Swindon,
1965–66. Administrative
and recreation centre
for the Fred Olsen Ltd.
shipping line, Millwall
Docks, London, 1968–69.

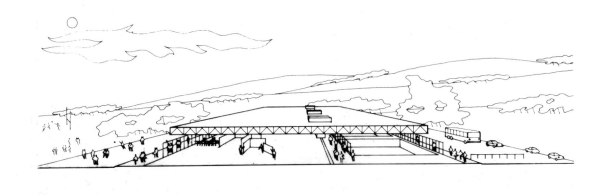

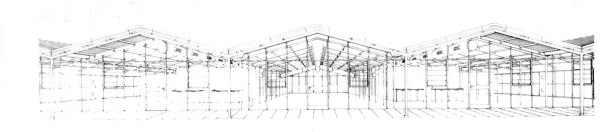

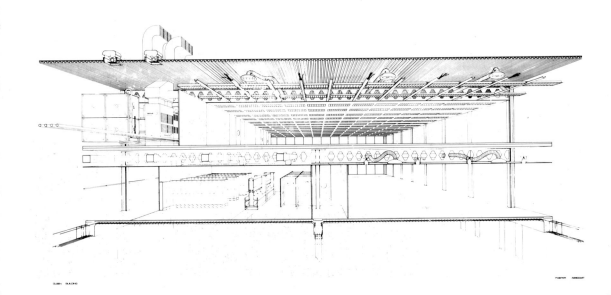

is a much more demanding standard than might initially appear. It requires the capacity for radical alteration in three important areas: the location of walls, air conditioning and the supply system. It must be possible to dismantle partitions as necessary and re-erect them elsewhere to create different spaces, which affects the floor plan as a whole. Air conditioning must be capable of adaptation to the changed spaces as well as to newly installed equipment and its very different requirements. The supply networks for building services must offer easy access at low cost and without impairment of function, and the corresponding arrangement of the supply systems brings considerable space demands for shafts and intermediate floors. The increasing speed of the transformation of requirements and possible solutions with respect to office equipment have rendered many buildings, some of them younger than this, obsolete and redundant.

In a lecture in the Pompidou Centre on February 26, 1981, Foster defined his understanding of flexibility by referring to one of his favourite areas: 'The question of flexibility is a search for defining the long-life parts and short-life parts of a building and has many parallels in aviation. The Jet Ranger helicopter for example was introduced in 1965, and although the technology of many of the units such as the engine and electronics has changed quite dramatically, it is still in production. Even though its appearance is that of a fixed object it is still subject to a process of continuous change. Unlike another kind of helicopter, the Bell 47, with its exposed structure which was subject to the same kind of change and looks meant for change; paradoxically it has been overtaken by events and is now out of production.' The remark is interesting because Foster is often regarded as designing for the sake of outward appearance. Some have gone so far as to deny him the rank of a 'true high-tech architect' because his buildings do not appear to have been designed for, or with the possibility of, change. Foster's remark makes the point: flexibility and the appearance of flexibility are two different things; if the architect's priority is function, the question of form goes far beyond the mere expression of function.

The headquarters of the Willis Faber & Dumas insurance company (1971–75) is famous for its technological innovations. Even if it is the visual effect of the mirror glass façade that it is chiefly associated with, its innovative significance lies in its structure. Glass works better when it is under tension, and a new type of suspended curtain wall was developed to take advantage of this characteristic. This is the first of Foster's projects in which prototypes were used for quality assurance, in the area of new technologies as well as with more traditional methods.

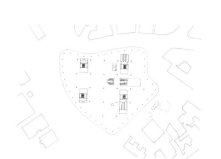

Headquarters of Willis Faber & Dumas, Ipswich, Suffolk, 1971–75. Second floor plan.

In the architects' opinion, Willis Faber & Dumas is distinguished above all by its quality as a workplace. The square vertical tower conventionally used for such office buildings was rejected: it would have sat uncomfortably in the traditional urban context of Ipswich, a small market town in the east of England. The completed building is comparatively low and uses the gentle curves of its façades to echo the twisting pattern of the medieval streets and to establish a connection between such different scales as the busy street on one side and the Unitarian Meeting House, with its aura of serenity, on the other. This solution results in a deep, supple building that uses the whole site to better advantage and consumes less energy. The rejection of conventional notions of office building space planning made it possible to build a swimming pool and rooftop garden, and the product was somewhat more joyful. Unlike most commercial buildings, special emphasis is placed on the effective design of the work areas rather than the thoroughfares: '. . . orientation is direct: you always know where you are, one can move freely, the sun penetrates everywhere, and there are only a few visual barriers.'[20] The upper storeys open like galleries onto a central atrium, where a bank of escalators forms a continuous path from the entrance to the restaurant in the roof garden. The correspondingly staggered openings in the intermediate floors combine to form an angled lightwell which also illuminates the office floors from inside. The effect is astonishing and offers employees and visitors an experience as pleasing as it is memorable.[21]

Willis Faber & Dumas is the first building that reveals the great architect. The synthesis of harmony and efficiency, the external image, the quality of the workplaces, the social components, the space, the light, the colour, the technological innovation, all these are combined with sophistication and intelligence. It remains one of the most beautiful achievements of Norman Foster.

[20] Foster would use very similar words to describe the Stansted Airport completed in 1991.

[21] In his lecture to the RIBA in 1983 Foster cited a remark by the director: the spatial plan had created good communications among the 1300 employees, who now exchanged greetings and farewells almost like members of a family, in stark contrast to the atmosphere in the old building with its elevators and corridors.

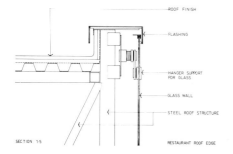

ROOF FINISH

FLASHING

HANGER SUPPORT
FOR GLASS

GLASS WALL

STEEL ROOF STRUCTURE

SECTION 1:5

RESTAURANT ROOF EDGE

Willis Faber & Dumas.
The building by day and
night. Detail of roof
parapet, top floor and
ground floor.

Buildings for the public

For Foster the 1970s was the period in which he was able to demonstrate his skill in the design of office and industrial buildings. But this period also offered him his first opportunity to build for the public. Two exemplary projects from this period are the Sainsbury Centre in Norwich, a gallery and School of Fine Art, and the scheme for the Hammersmith Centre for the London Transport Executive. These commissions opened up the possibility of using principles from commercial construction in new building types. This shift in the challenges to be met allowed Foster to enrich his repertoire and to design on a larger scale.

THE SAINSBURY CENTRE

The Sainsbury Centre for the Visual Arts, completed in 1978, owes its existence to the decision of Sir Robert and Lady Sainsbury to donate their art collection to the University of East Anglia in Norwich. The donors, rather than creating a museum in the traditional sense, wanted to offer students the opportunity of experiencing art at any time during their daily work. For Foster this assignment meant creating, in a dimension new for him, a fruitful mixture of the most varied spheres of activity: an exhibition space, rooms for the teaching of art history and public areas were to be brought together.

As with the commercial buildings, Foster proposed combining all these functions under a unified skin in a large flexible space. From the very first sketches, the plans envisaged a linear arrangement of the most important spaces in a simple volume. Foster explored a variety of structural systems, but when the project was already well under way he made a decisive change. The traditional front and side halls were replaced by an integrated three-dimensional solution: all services and auxiliary rooms were placed in a deep, steel truss framework which comprised both the roof and the side walls, wrapping around the long internal space like a protective shell. Sanitary installations, kitchen, laboratories, etc. are randomly distributed within the framework and can be rearranged at any time, independently from its inner and outer panels. An extraordinary simplicity of internal organization was achieved by placing workshops and storerooms in a kind of spine in the basement and placing two open mezzanines across the width of the structure as the only defining elements for the different functional areas.

In his lecture to the Royal Institute of British Architects Foster declared that light is the central theme of the Sainsbury Centre. In fact, light has a lot to do with the all-enclosing spatial skin. The ceiling beneath the partially glazed roof is formed by long, aluminum louvres mechanically controlled by light sensors inside and outside the building. These louvres enable minute and perfect control of the

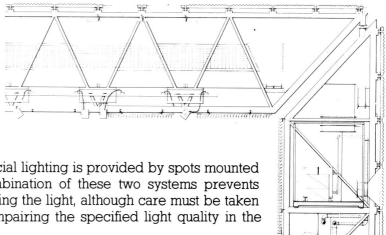

quality of light inside. Artificial lighting is provided by spots mounted on a rail system. The combination of these two systems prevents infinite possibilities for varying the light, although care must be taken to prevent daylight from impairing the specified light quality in the exhibition gallery.

The two completely glazed gable ends of the building are like immaterial membranes, and the building appears capable of infinite expansion on its longitudinal axis, particularly since all the cladding panels on its sides are interchangeable. The building already suggests parallels with the Pompidou Centre, designed and completed between 1971 and 1977 by Richard Rogers and Renzo Piano. Apart from the special character of the Paris building, which was conditioned by its size and its position in the urban environment, the basic design strategy is the same. The differences in implementation, however, show all the more clearly why Foster and Rogers went their separate ways: while the skin of the Pompidou Centre is de-emphasized by the exposure of the structure and the visible flowing streams of its occupants, the Sainsbury Centre concentrates all its services in a skin that is expressive as well as compact and unified, revealing a variety of graphic and plastic qualities in changing daylight. Its almost monochrome, grey-and-white patterns of plane, line and space give the building the appearance of a splendid palimpsest, while in Paris a sensational composition of structural forms and huge pipes is picked out by bright primary colours, to each of which a particular function is assigned. But in Paris as in Norwich, the designs are based on the same methods of construction: extensive pre-fabrication in the factory limits work on site to the assembly of the pre-fabricated components and to the pouring of foundations and sub-floors. Foster's external cladding panels, with their clearly visible joints that serve neatly as rainwater gutters, are rightly considered one of the most characteristic examples of his relationship to structure.

Sainsbury Centre under construction, structural detail.
Following pages: overall view.

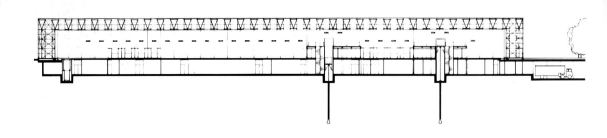

Norman Foster with
Buckminster Fuller:
autonomous house, 1982,
not built.

Norman Foster with
Buckminster Fuller:
Samuel Beckett Theatre,
St Peter's College,
Oxford, 1971, not built.

BUCKMINSTER
FULLER

During a visit to the construction site, Buckminster Fuller asked Foster about the weight of the building. When the calculations were produced they confirmed the supposition of the famous American philospher, architect and mathematician: the concrete basement, which was only 8% of the total volume, accounted for 80% of the building's weight; the construction costs for the basement were only 50% less, and the construction time roughly twice as long, as for the main part of the building, which takes up roughly 72% of the total volume. Moreover, as Foster noted, the basement turned out poorly in comparison with the main building.

Thus we come to a favourite idea of Foster's: the relationship between weight, energy and performance – to which Foster himself would add 'joy'.[22]

[22] Lecture in the Pompidou Centre, 1981.

Towards the end of his life Buckminster Fuller became a friend of Norman Foster. Until his death in 1983 he was an important adviser in whom Foster had complete confidence. Foster first worked with Fuller in 1971, when the American received a commission to produce a scheme for an experimental theatre at St Peter's College in Oxford. Foster assisted in this project, which Fuller designed as an underground multi-functional hall intended to serve as a classroom and exhibition space. When Foster in return then solicited Fuller's advice on the Willis Faber & Dumas project, Fuller proposed a large skin of the type he had developed for his own projects, such as the Climatron in St Louis or the dome at the Expo in Montreal: light, transparent domes that allowed the creation of internal micro-climates. Foster developed this idea 'further under the name Climatroffice, as one of the few projects – along with the 'autonomous house' conceived jointly with Fuller – in which Foster explored more or less utopian paths. The Climatroffice enabled Foster to radicalize ideas already present in his work and to integrate them – once developed further – into projects that would be executed later: flexibility of use; reducing energy consumption; enclosure of the greatest possible space with the smallest area of skin; lightness; as much natural light as possible; and finally 'perfect space', in which, amid a pleasant atmosphere, 'all changes are possible with elegance and without exertion'.[23]

[23] Lecture More with Less, 1979.

HAMMERSMITH
CENTRE

For Foster the Hammersmith Centre was a project on a new scale, a first encounter with the world of public authority clients and the first opportunity to design facilities for a wider public. The site in the London borough of Hammersmith is one of the most congested traffic intersections in Europe. London Transport wished to create new bus stops and a new interchange for bus and underground. This required

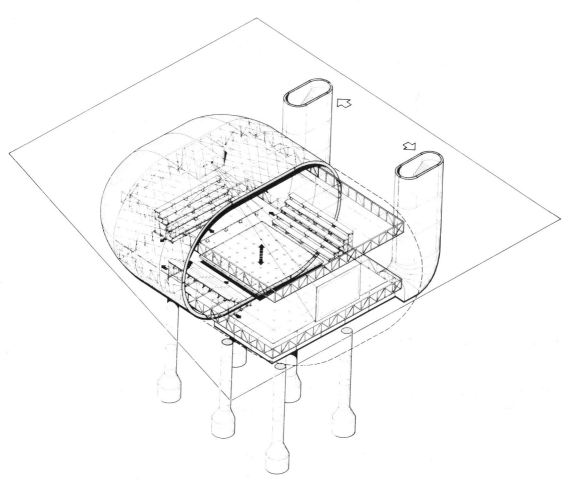

Norman Foster with
Buckminster Fuller:
Climatroffice, project
1971, not built.

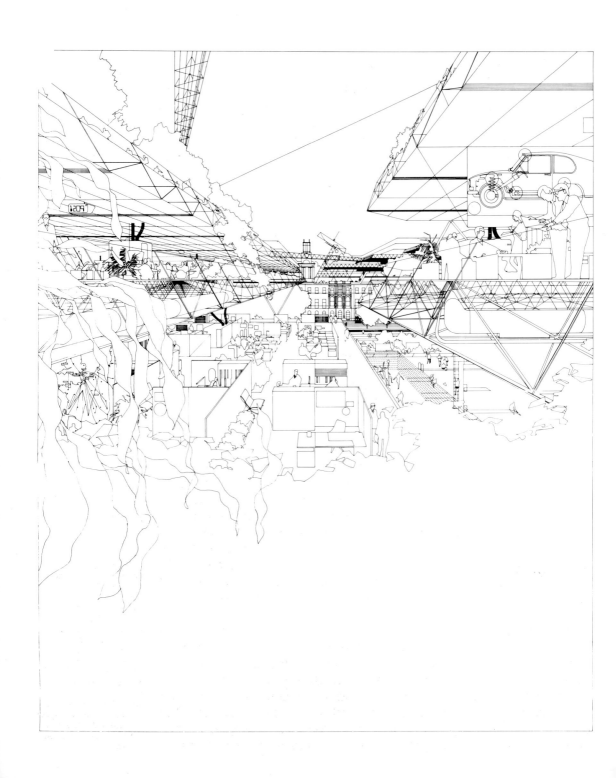

subsidizing by a speculative office development, and a permit to do so was granted.

Foster's first step was a detailed study of the site and its history. At the same time he used a series of models to test different plans and possibilities for space and mass. This soon led to the idea of returning to the pre-industrial urban form, with construction above the transport facilities in the form of a ring of buildings encircling a large garden. This solution implied a linear arrangement of the offices which in turn enabled a conventional building depth. The open space in the centre was roughly the area of Trafalgar Square (about 1.5 ha), but the cultivated atmosphere more closely corresponded to London's elegant residential squares such as Cavendish, Manchester or Berkeley. Two distinct levels emerged in the course of the design: the base and, above it, the ring, with different heights and in some cases with an open intermediate space to connect the central square with the public park that the architects planned beside the neighbouring church. The next phase addressed the ensemble as a whole and smoothed out the idiosyncrasies, particularly in the vertical movement; the heights were set to an identical scale. To articulate the huge façades, Foster sought a conspicuous solution for the access points. The final scheme envisaged four blocks of office accommodation forming the ring, connected at the four corners by 'gateways' in the form of double towers with transparent cladding which would house the services and create a formal allusion – in some of the models – to the pointed towers of the neighbouring church.

At the same time the team conceived the plan of a protective canopy above the central area. Made of transparent material, it would solve a whole series of climatic problems, and the savings in energy would overwhelmingly compensate for the cost of construction. This type of canopy also created many new architectural possibilities: life in the Mediterranean city has always seduced the British architect, and here was a place in the centre of London where this dream could become a reality! It is significant that the illustrative sketches now suddenly show a completely different image, bubbling over with life and activity.

The departure of the chairman of London Transport and the decision to ignore the British developers, several of whom were well-disposed to Foster's proposals, in favour of the Dutch company Bredero, brought the project to a halt in 1979 after two years of work.[24] Foster had designed the blocks 18 m deep – which was realistic and is standard today – but Bredero insisted on the then standard 12 m and advocated changing the plan into a series of T-shaped blocks, which completely destroyed the effect of the large public space.

[24] "... (F)irst of all the undertaking had to be financially balanced, although no public money was available; second, the centre had to function as a connection between the underground and the omnibus lines; and finally it had to do something for the community, it had 'to work for the people'" Foster in his lecture to the RIBA in 1983). The architect was reluctant to drop a project that had met with almost universal approval among citizens.

Hammersmith Centre for
London Transport, 1977–
79, not built. Plan of
standard floor, section,
model of the whole
complex and of a pair of
towers.

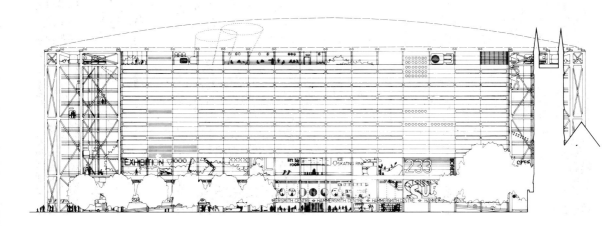

Clients and architect were unable to come to agreement. Thus Hammersmith joined the long series of projects that exist only on paper.

ATHLETICS
HALL,
FRANKFURT

Two years after the failure of Hammersmith, Foster undertook another project that would prove equally disappointing: an indoor stadium in Frankfurt. The story began with a competition in which Foster was the only foreign architect to be invited to participate. In his first attempt Foster tried to preserve as many of the trees as possible on the site as well as to exercise a certain restraint, so that the neighbouring buildings would not be overpowered. The scheme recessed the stadium into the ground and covered it with a flat roof.[25] After a variety of structural and roof systems had been tested, a cost analysis finally showed that a low vault, similar to that of an aircraft hangar, was the optimum solution. Instead of conventional arcs, Foster proposed an elegant lattice structure consisting of intersecting hexagons and triangles. The scheme is a development of the Sainsbury Centre in Norwich, yet the curving skin, in which once again structural and supply elements as well as natural and artificial lighting are integrated, has become much thinner.

[25] The excavations in the ground, described as 'organic' by Foster, were soon continued in the mussel-shaped vaulted roof, which equally recalled Frank Lloyd Wright.

On September 17, 1981 Foster and his team were awarded the first prize. Yet the city of Frankfurt organized a second round, not provided for in the competition conditions, between Foster and the winner of the second prize, the Braun and Schlockermann group. The following months saw development of the projecting canopy over the entrance, one of Foster's most beautiful inspirations. In the spring of 1982 Foster Associates won the second round of the competition, with a scheme very similar to the first proposal. After a long period of indecision, the client returned to the project in the autumn of 1985 and appointed Foster, together with Braun and Schlockermann as the supervising architects. Then after political changes and new excuses from the client, the project was finally cancelled in favour of another sports centre. Thus one of Foster's most beautiful projects came to an ignominious end. Although the number of commissions grew steadily, and despite his international recognition, the architect repeatedly suffered blows or was compelled to abandon projects: the Humana Tower in 1982, BBC in 1983, Televisa and Nancy in 1986, the Paternoster, Turin and The Hague in 1987 – all projects that emerged from the work of the early 1970s.

In this period, which greatly enriched the scope of Foster's work and his creative power, the ideas developed by Buckminster Fuller – the pre-fabricated capsule, the geodesic dome – as well as Foster's interests in such subjects as the Airstream aluminium trailer and

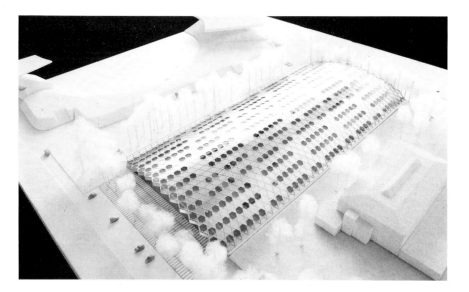

Athletics stadium in Frankfurt, 1981–86, not built. Models of roof structure and cladding.

Athletics stadium in Frankfurt. Schematic sketch.

gliders and their lightweight structures, all find expression in the public buildings of Sainsbury, Hammersmith and Frankfurt. These buildings' innovative force makes them a high point in Foster's work. In addition to their technological themes, they increasingly reveal touches of other models that had once served as references for modernist orthodoxy, but had since been neglected: the glass house of Chareau (1931), the traditional Japanese house, traditional solutions for the transition between inside and outside,[26] and above all the iron architecture of nineteenth-century England, with its punctuated arches, its large glazed roofs and its huge flowing spaces. The corn exchange in the north of England with a central three-storey atrium, skylit and surrounded by long galleries, was soon overtaken in importance by the big train stations, by the Galleria Vittorio Emanuele II in Milan, and above all by the Crystal Palace of 1851. Certainly Paxton's building forms a technical point of reference with its concept of comprehensive pre-fabrication, its countless small identical components and its technological optimism and empiricism. But it also presupposed immense architectural experience: the iron and glass construction afforded a huge interior space, which contained several hundred-year-old oaks and was flooded with natural light.

All these features are subtly present in Foster's large public works and will return in the later projects, no matter what their programme. They set Norman Foster a clear distance from the fashion that began to rule architecture at the end of the 1970s. Not only does his work bear no relationship to post-modernism, which arose in the United States in the middle of the 1960s, but it also differs distinctly from the fashion of 'high tech'. In the middle of the 1980s Foster was to explain: 'I don't know what "high tech" means: it conceals a stylistic idea shaped by fashion, and I distrust that. Some of the techniques that we use during construction are not new. To a certain degree our point of view has its origin in the nineteenth century. Attitudes then, whether to planning or implementation, were very different from today's. They borrowed freely from all possible sources ... It was a much more global approach.'[27]

[26] Foster's interest in such traditional structures manifested itself for the first time in 1975 in his regional studies for the Canary Islands. In his presentations to the Sainsbury Centre client, for example, he referred to the Casba.

[27] Quoted according to the jacket text of *Norman Foster*, Electa-Moniteur, Paris 1986.

Design philosophy

Several of Foster's projects from the period of the high tech fashion seem to participate in this movement. Pursuing the line of development begun with the previous projects, Foster designed sensational buildings such as the Renault Distribution Centre in Swindon (1980–82), the Hongkong Bank (1979–86) and various furniture designs (1981, 1983, 1987). All these projects use large amounts of steel and emphasize the structure as demonstratively as the buildings of Mies van der Rohe, in a style that appears to indicate a turning point in Foster's work. In fact his previous 'minimalism' was relinquished in favour of a demonstration of the structure which brought Foster closer to Rogers and Piano, who were striving in turn toward 'structural expressionism'. In other buildings, however, Foster maintained his search for the perfect skin and an architectural idiom pared to an absolute minimum. The more recent buildings, from the beginning of the 1990s, show this tendency and it would probably be correct to identify two aspirations in his work: one that gives priority to structure, the other to the skin. These aspirations are co-equal and co-exist, at times even coinciding, and they are used by Foster as the major alternatives for each project, depending on the conditions specified by the brief.

The computer centre for IBM in Greenford, one of the biggest in Europe, was completed in 1978–79 in just eight months. The first stage of construction combined functions that were widely different from each other, just as in Foster's earlier commercial buildings. In Greenford, however, he introduced a clear distinction between the glazed curtain walls and the long unbroken expanses of ribbed claddings – an arrangement that would create a furor lasting for years. As at IBM Cosham, the extreme austerity of the façade design is attained by setting the structure back behind the cladding and stretching a smooth, uninterrupted skin from the ground to the eaves. There is virtually no external indication of the roof structure.

IBM AND RENAULT

Renault required a building that would promote a strong corporate image for their Distribution Centre in Swindon. There were also very precise constraints on schedules and financing[28] and a need for internal flexibility. To meet these different criteria, the selected solution was based on a structural module that would facilitate later expansion. Standard 24 m^2 modules are suspended from 16 m masts, with an eaves height of 7.5 m and a ridge height of 9.5 m. The first completed section consists of 42 modules arranged on a simple grid that encompasses 10 000 m^3. Each row becomes shortened, however, toward the front side. The warehouse is a rectangle 9 modules long by 4 modules wide; the width is stepped down at the southern end

[28] The building cost around £8.5 million (1983 value).

to 3 modules with the service areas – offices, a restaurant and a school – then the show room takes up two modules and finally the huge entrance canopy is one module square. The schematic simplicity of the ground plan, as so often with Foster, is accompanied by extraordinary technical sophistication in the treatment of the structure as well as of the skin. Despite their precisely detailed differentiation, all elements of the structure harmonize with each other and give a distinct sense of unity to the living building with its gently vaulted roof.

NEO-PRODUCTIVISM

In all of Foster's work the architectural form has a direct relationship with standardized production and with function. The 'design' has its origin primarily in the process of production and assembly. This emphasis on fabrication has led Kenneth Frampton to speak of 'neo-productivism' in respect to Foster. And yet, as Frampton says, Foster should not be confused with the Russian productivism of the 1920s, even if his way of seeing and working recalls Tatlin's dictum: 'The material creates the technique and the technique creates the form.' In fact Tatlin and the Russian cubo-futurists brought construction to the forefront in order to replace that classic conception of the traditional art world, 'composition'. Art had to progress from the contemplative passivity of the composition; one should not simply ponder the world, but rather 'construct' it unhindered.

This dichotomy of construction and composition explains Foster's practice of creating an entire series of alternative compositions for each project. In so doing he establishes a strategy in which the various alternatives are evaluated in terms of 'for' and 'against', which is as essential for the design as for negotiations with the client. No composition emerges from a particular preconception or prejudice, whatever its form. Instead, the development of each composition leads to the evolution of a strict hierarchy among its various elements. For example, during projects in which construction is the key element of the architectural concept, all other elements become subordinate. This applies regardless of the material of which the building will be constructed, whether it be steel in the case of the Renault building, or concrete in the case of an expressive arch system for the Televisa Project in Mexico (1986). For this hierarchy is of an aesthetic nature and it has nothing in common with constructivist theory. Fundamentally it belongs to the realm of composition; and yet it remains reconcilable with the new 'productivism' followed by Foster, which demands that the forms should be derived from production.

Theoretically the 'product forms' would have to appear every-

Distribution centre for
Renault UK Ltd., Swindon,
Wiltshire, 1980–83. Aerial
view of the complex.

Renault Distribution
Centre, corner detail,
model of the entrance
zone.

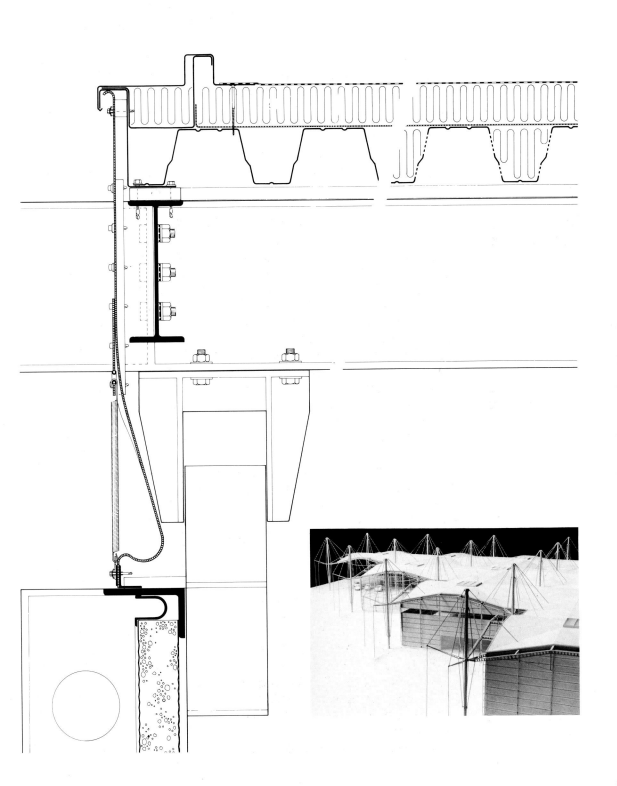

Radio and television
tower for Televisa,
Mexico, 1986, not built.
Photographs of models.

where in regular monotony. This, in essence, is characteristic of the works of Rogers, especially for Lloyd's of London, frequently compared by critics with the Hongkong Bank, Foster's masterpiece of the 1980s. But while in Foster's case the service modules and risers are closely interlinked to the point that they can hardly be distinguished individually, and moreover incontrovertibly give priority to the structure, the supply centres and service shafts on the façades designed by Rogers are immediately recognizable as such. Foster generally avoids making use of service systems for architectural purposes. This is evident even in the case of the Hongkong Bank, which is characterized inside and out by the same sense of hierarchy and which is clearly dominated by that which, beyond this productivism, is the practical objective of architecture: space. Foster's buildings, whether they emphasize the structure or not, clearly show what they owe to the form of production; what cannot be traced to that source is determined by the organization of space. While Norman Foster 'cultivates the detail', he is above all a great creator of spaces.

'NO DETAIL IS TOO SMALL'

In his striving for quality Foster attempts to refine the normal, indeed unconscious experience of everyday life – not with luxurious materials, but rather through extreme care in the handling of different materials, all the way down to the tactile quality of the details. The architect says, 'It is a personal belief that quality is an attitude of mind and quite independent of the actual materials in question – whether brick, concrete, wood, paper, steel, aluminium, stone or precious metal. It is more a matter of respect and loving care, whether on-site or on the factory floor.'[29] Foster often uses the expression 'loving care' in respect of materials and craftsmanship. For him this 'remains just as valid today as earlier, even though the work on the construction site is increasingly becoming replaced by the assembly of prefabricated elements.'[30] Before beginning his training in architecture, Foster worked in the Town Hall in Manchester. In this wonderful building by Waterhouse it was precisely the details that impressed him most: the handrails of the balustrades, the lamps, even the glass-sided water cisterns in the toilets. From his service with the Royal Air Force Foster has retained a love of aircraft, of their simple and efficient forms. It is here, in heliostats or the aerodynamic trailers, for example, that he finds the perfection of precise harmony with barely visible junctions between strictly hierarchically organized components.

[29] Norman Foster, 'Prologue', in: Process Architecture, no. 70, Sept. 1986, p. 9.

[30] Norman Foster, 'Hongkong Bank', in A & U, no. 189, June 1986, p. 25.

'DESIGN DEVELOPMENT'

Foster accepts that it is impossible for the architect of today to be totally conversant with the technology of construction. But he rejects the suggestion that the architect should therefore take a passive role. His intention is to retain control over forms and materials. This purpose is served by 'design development', a kind of working collaboration between industry and the architect. Within this demanding framework all traditional distinctions between the tasks of the architect and those of the engineer are suspended.

The methods available to the team extend from the development of a completely new system, through the modification of existing products to the use of standardized elements ordered from catalogues. Design development evolved from the need for speed, low costs and high quality; it pursues the difficult aim of reconciling these three requirements. Here cooperation between administrators, quantity surveyors, structural engineers and many other specialists plays a crucial role. Coordination and communication are essential for success: architects and engineers, for example, must work together constantly. The close links between Foster and Ove Arup and Partners, the structural engineers, are a matter of general knowledge. Sir Norman Foster and Partners also employ several engineers.

Equally essential in the process of design development is that the proposals of the team are coordinated with the building contractor and the clients – from the very first phase of design wherever possible. To this end, all types of graphic presentation are used to visualize the scheme, for communication is easier with drawings than with words. It is the three-dimensional version that forms the basis of design development – for example, in the form of spatial models, prototypes and full-scale mock-ups in card or plastic. Design development is a process distinguished by prudence and carefulness. It may seem laborious or even self-fulfilling, but in comparison to other industries, such as automobile production or aerospace, its advantages are still not appreciated, and this can be dangerous – for, as Foster says, 'With a building you have a chance, but only one chance.'

COMPONENT CONSTRUCTION

There was a time when designers assumed that to apply a progressive technology to construction necessitated the standardization of components and therefore also of the buildings. Foster's first works illustrated the fallacy of this.

The tower of the Hongkong Bank represents a further step away from this perception of standardization, for virtually every single element in it was created especially for this project.

This building has two particularly striking characteristics. First, there is the large number of shapes and sizes of panels: even if the panels are duplicated to a certain degree, this is not exactly standardization. Second, there is the faultless workmanship – no distortions, no welding on the cladding, no deformations at the junctions. This is partly due to the thickness of the aluminium, but the real secret involved the use of electronically controlled robots in the production process. These machines can handle extremely complex geometric tasks whose analysis alone would take months without a computer.[31] The Hongkong Bank is the first of a new generation of buildings in which relatively small quantities of structural elements were produced to order by robots. Electronic technology from the aerospace industry made this possible at costs comparable to those of large volume production. It is by no means presumptuous to suggest that the technology and the refinement of the summit of achievement represented by the Hongkong Bank will set a precedent in the world of construction and usher in a new era.

[31] Cf. Colin Davies, 'Building the Bank', in: *The Architectural Review*, No. 1070, April 1986.

The overcoming of monotony and repetition provided by the introduction of 'intelligent' robots into the production process goes, for Foster, hand in hand with a transformation of his design procedure. Although 'productivism' remains as his basis, Foster nonetheless stresses that his method is more intuitive than anything else and that directly human aspects, such as the quality of light or the hierarchy of spaces, have the same priority as the means of production: 'In general it is the technology that people notice in our buildings. But this is an area in which quality ought to be self-evident! What makes the difference is the site, the relationship to the environment and to people. The efforts of the architect are questionable when no emotion is involved; the function of architecture does not exhaust itself in renovating and covering. Each project must be begun with the desire to stimulate a movement of the spirit. It is one of the tasks of the architect to transform and refine banal everyday experience, and this has to do with feelings, not with science fiction.'[32]

[32] From a conversation with the author in January 1988.

When Foster opened his new office in Great Portland Street in London in 1981, it appeared that the only way he would obtain furniture meeting his requirements was by designing it as a system of his own.[33] Though he had already drawn up a study for an English furniture manufacturer, Foster now embarked on a genuine adventure: the creation of 'Foster furniture'.

The office was a kind of show window for Foster Associates. Models, prototypes and photographs provided an overview of Norman Foster's architectural philosophy. The furniture office had

FURNITURE

[33] "For ourselves we could not find anything that would work as a drawing board to our satisfaction. They were either too heavy, too clumsy, too expensive, we did not like the way they looked and you could not move them around." Lecture at MoMA, New York, November 1982.

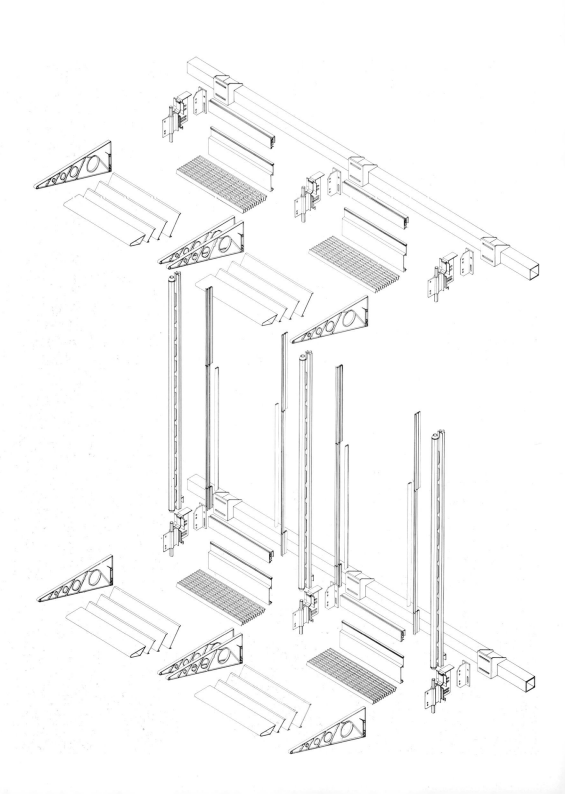

Component construction:
connecting walkways on
the façade of the
Hongkong Bank.
Exploded view and
section of façade.

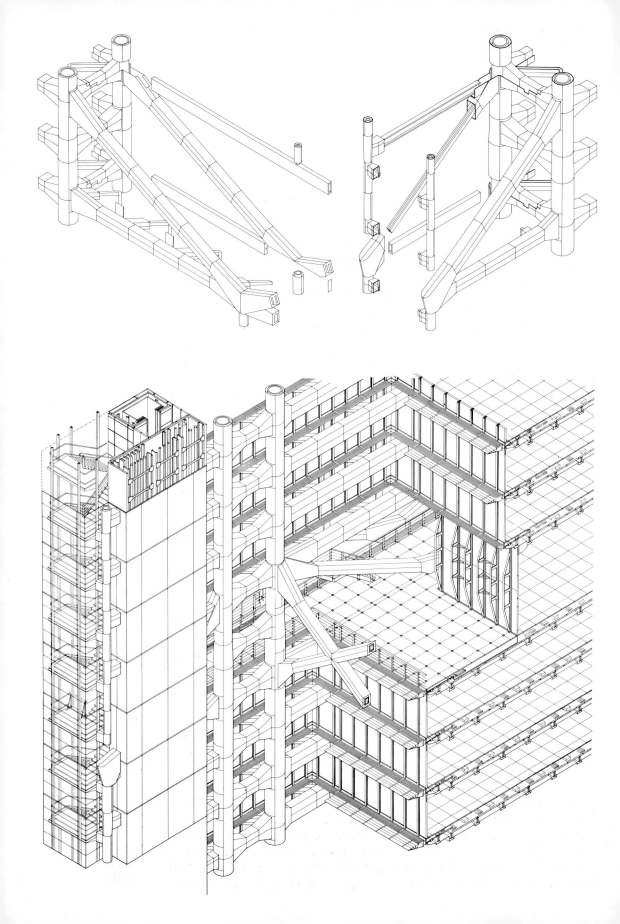

to be tailored to suit both the atmosphere of the office and the designs created here. It had to be light, both in weight and in appearance, as well as very flexible. The table legs, for example, had to be capable of folding for easy transport. A multi-jointed mechanism allowed the table tops to be raised and fixed at any angle, so that they could be used for all purposes, even as poster displays or exhibition stands. Great attention was paid to the adjustable-height foot component, whose short vertical tube and disc recall the Lunar Module developed by NASA. Other inspirations for the furniture system were the X-shaped chassis of the Lotus racing car, created by Colin Chapman, with its simple frame on which various elements can be mounted, and the typical 'dentist's chair', which also fascinated Foster. Although special attention was paid to the drawing tables, they were regarded from the outset as one element in a much larger system: they are based on the principle of a tube-shaped spine to which a wide variety of elements can be connected in many configurations. Thus, for example, a table may be combined with a low supporting element, which can then be connected in turn to a typing stand. Like the table itself, the entire system is extremely flexible and offers a wide variety of components. The principle of the central spine made the drawing tables the basis of a comprehensive component system that allowed modification according to the particular needs of any user.

The parallel commission for the furniture of the Renault building offered an opportunity for further development. The basic table became a restaurant table with a glass top. It was joined by a round table and a type of simple reception desk developed from earlier studies. But since the quantity of furniture to be produced was relatively small, the manufacturing process did not undergo any further refinement: welding was the main fabrication method, and little effort was made to minimize the number of joints.

Foster's collaboration with the Italian company Tecno fundamentally changed the nature of the problem. Even if there is a certain similarity to his earlier furniture, Nomos nonetheless represents a collection of new products designed in close cooperation with the manufacturer from the beginning.

TECNO

The large number of welding points on the furniture for Renault ruled out economical production on an industrial scale. Instead cast aluminium parts were developed to connect the steel elements. As was to be expected, only an Italian manufacturer proved capable of carrying out the industrial production of this furniture. In the 1970s Italy had given birth to a furniture industry that worked by a system of

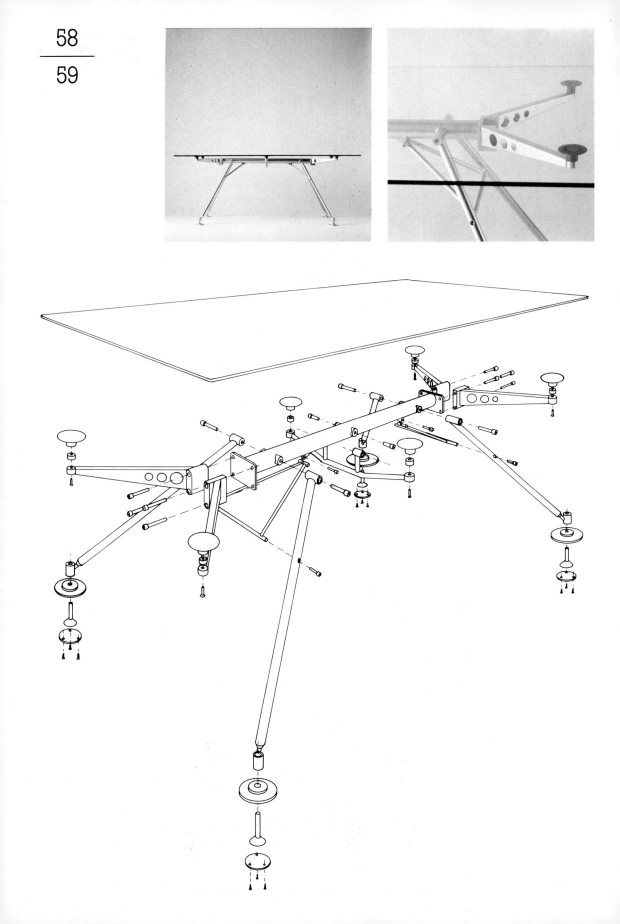

Furniture systems.
Opposite top: table from
the furniture series
designed for Renault.
Below: exploded
drawing.

Drawing table frame
folded down; in horizontal
position; raised.

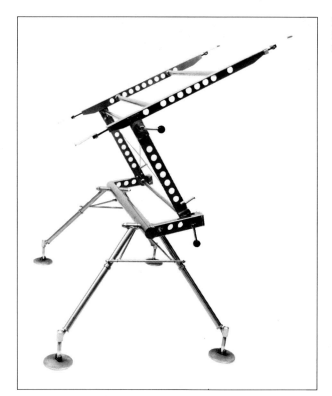

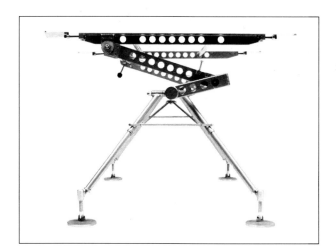

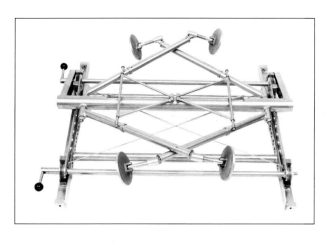

contractual relationships between small, specialized companies. These firms offered highly skilled traditional artisans working with ultra-modern, electronically controlled equipment. All this enabled great flexibility, allowed more rapid innovation than in a centralized industry, and offered in addition a high degree of *savoir faire*.

Tecno has an especially good reputation for the production of cast aluminium parts. For 25 years the company has worked with a small foundry near Brescia. With its 140 employees, the Cervati Foundry produces work for a large body of international customers, but, in accordance with the wishes of Tecno, does not collaborate with any other furniture manufacturers. This understanding and the numerous visits of the Cervati engineers to Tecno factories have led to a remarkable quality of product. The complex high-pressure casting processes necessary to mass-produce furniture parts at reasonable costs require specialized equipment.[34] However simple it may be to drill a hole through a section of tubing and to weld another section to it, it is inordinately difficult to produce the same construction in volume – particularly when this section of tubing is the most important part in an entire component system.

NOMOS

The Tecno products designed by Foster Associates include a series of tables and an office system. The main difference between the two is in the configuration of the upper frame: while the table's legs, struts and the slanting cantilevers that support the top function together as individual elements, the office system uses a three-dimensional framework; it also supports a superstructure on top of which an uplighter is mounted.[35] It is these features that characterize each series: in the case of the table, the cantilevers are anchored under the spine and the spine is diagonally braced by the legs; in the office system, the supporting frame and superstructure are continuous and the table top extends either side of the superstructure. The assignment of the three basic elements – the spine, the feet and the superstructure on the one hand and the cantilevers on the other – all clearly distinguished and hierarchically arranged,[36] follows in any case an unusual geometry more reminiscent of an animal's bone structure. For, in fact, all the articulations are clear and explicit, even if they are jointed in an extremely complex way.

Foster's table, in all its variants, calls to mind a spaceship, due to the way it rests on the ground as if supported on springs; but it is also reminiscent of a crossbow, with tubing, arms and struts combining to form an object filled with tension. Other images and comparisons are also invoked: the grasshopper that spreads its graceful legs wide

[34] The director of Tecno, Marco Fantoni, offered this laconic commentary on the significant investment costs: "It is better to spend an extra pound on the machinery than an extra penny on each component produced." Cf. Penny Sparke, 'Architecture in Miniature', in: *Norman Foster, Buildings and Projects*, ed. Ian Lambot, Vol. 3, 1989.

[35] In contrast to the conventional non-technical solution, the power cables are not hidden, but rather mounted visibly in a kind of 'spinal cord' consisting of two types of ring.

[36] The table system is characterized by a hierarchy between the elements of the frame, while the office system incorporates many mounts and the structure of the frame is consistently simplified.

when resting, or the cockpit of a modern jet, whose controls are not restricted to a single surface but are distributed all around within easy reach. Foster's experience as a pilot may have played a role in this profound re-configuration of the workplace. For that is probably the main contribution of the Tecno series, going beyond the plastic beauty of the table itself, which will undoubtedly become a classic: the 'desk' has been transformed into a spatial object. By arranging all things within reach without impairing the field of view, but off the table top, the desk is no longer a storage area and is freed for use as a true workplace.

Furniture system for
Tecno, 1985–87.

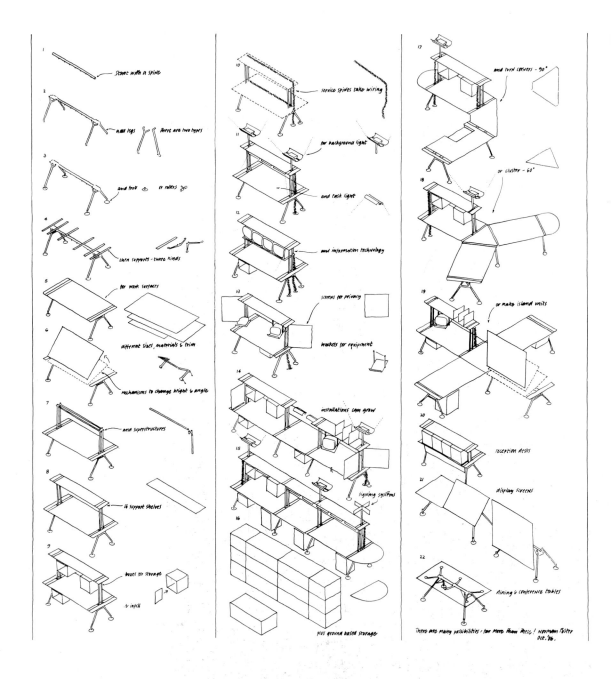

1 Start with a spine

2 and legs / There are two types

3 and feet / or rollers

4 then supports - three kinds

5 for work surfaces

6 different sizes, materials & trim / mechanisms to change height & angle

7 and superstructures

8 & support shelves

9 boxes for storage / & infill

10 service spines take wiring

11 for background light / and task light

12 and information technology

13 screens for privacy / brackets for equipment

14 installations can grow

15 signing systems

16 plus ground based storage

17 and turn corners - 90°

18 or cluster - 60°

19 or make island units

20 reception desks

21 display screens

22 dining & conference tables

There are many possibilities - far more than these! Norman Foster
Oct. '86.

Nomos furniture system for Tecno. Combination of several tables with top-mounted uplight.

The history of an extraordinary project

In April 1986 the Hongkong and Shanghai Bank opened its new headquarters. It is a building of unusual charm which contains virtually no standard construction elements; its components were all developed from scratch. It is also a building that emphasizes the outstanding position occupied by the Chinese–British territory as a whole and by the corporation itself (the most important bank of the Far East and the central bank of Hong Kong) in the international financial world. The Bank is of vital importance for the functioning of the colony in the difficult period until the year 1997, when Hong Kong will be returned to China, and it fulfills its role in one of the most expensive buildings in the world, thus also demonstrating complete confidence in the future of Hong Kong.

Norman Foster received the commission as the outsider in a shortlist consisting almost exclusively of experienced skyscraper architects. His most important building to date, the headquarters of Willis Faber & Dumas, had three upper storeys; the Hongkong Bank was to have 47 storeys and stand 180 m high.

THE
COMPETITION

The history of the project begins with a meeting between the competing architects and the representatives of the Bank and its advisers. While the other architects returned to their home countries, Foster decided to cancel a planned vacation in order to spend the three weeks with his wife and his long-time companion Spencer de Grey studying the workings of the Bank, the surrounding area and the spirit of the site.

For its new administrative headquarters – situated, as the previous ones, on one of the most outstanding sites in the business centre since the founding of the colony – the Bank desired a building that would vividly express its dominant position in the colony while at the same time taking into account the requirements of the modern banking industry: it would have to accommodate the technical developments of the next 50 years without difficulty. Foster also placed great emphasis on meeting stringent requirements with respect to public life and the site's environment. For this reason he commissioned the building in London of a detailed model of the surrounding area, in order to check his various schemes in their urban context.[37]

37 A main problem that accompanied the entire design process proved to be the narrow Bank Street to the east of the property, where a façade structure of the greatest possible openness was required. The solution was finally found in the distinctive lamella structure of the building.

An existing study proposed different strategies for organizing and implementing the transition from the old building to the new one. These strategies proved unsatisfactory, however, because although they preserved the old office tower during the first phases of construction, they required the demolition of the main banking hall, which was a symbolic and popular part of the old administrative headquarters. Foster Associates worked out a more cautious variant

First studies for a
construction above the
hall of the old Hongkong
Bank building, 1979.

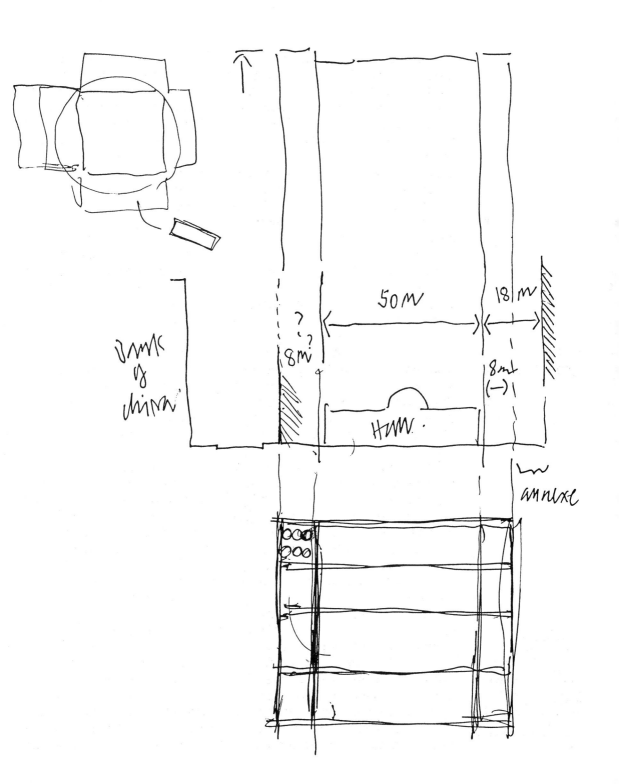

which essentially retained the vaulted hall but not the old northern tower.

The hall was to be enclosed by the new building. The sketch, which shows a schematic cross-section of this hallway placed in a large bridge construction, already contains in its few lines the basic concept of the future tower. This design idea opened up an abundance of possibilities: it would simplify the organization of the construction phases, but above all it would overcome the traditional high-rise floor plan[38] with its central supply core by shifting the service shafts to the external walls. The result was a hollowed-out building with office floors freed from any type of vertical barrier, making them extremely flexible. This strategy promised the Bank an impressive architectural image, both as a semi-public institution and as a commercial concern. Moreover, it gave the architect the initiative *vis-à-vis* the client and his advisers – a not insignificant psychological advantage.

The preliminary scheme for the competition was submitted in October 1979. The service shafts on the simple, quadratic plan are connected east to west by three rows of gigantic trusses from which the floor zones are hung. The open façades provide panoramic views. The alignment of the building effectively exploits the powerful north–south axis, with the city's harbour and the mountains, and the relationship to Statue Square on the north side is emphasized by a large hall conceived as a public space. The scheme also aims at absolute flexibility of the office levels through, for example, the general use of suspended floors, hitherto used only for rooms housing computer systems; thus, they are designed to contain the horizontal distribution of all the building's services. In their efforts to achieve maximum flexibility within the structure of a skyscraper the architects were led to rethink the functional and social value of conventional high rise offices and the problem of how to create more appropriate workplaces for the service sector.

When the schemes had been submitted, those involved soon came to the general opinion that Foster's design far outshone the others. After a long session of the Bank's board – the longest, it is said, in the corporation's history – the Chairman of the Hongkong and Shanghai Bank received a unanimous vote and declared Foster Associates the winner of the selection process.

[38] "This social, visual, and functional irritation" (Norman Foster).

THE 'CHEVRON' DESIGN

From that moment great speed was required. According to Foster, four basic principles made it possible to complete such a complex and demanding project in the short period of roughly six years: 'Firstly, the site would be more an assembly point than a building site

Models for competition
entry.

Early scheme
incorporating old bank
building. Cross-sections
of both buildings in their
urban environment.

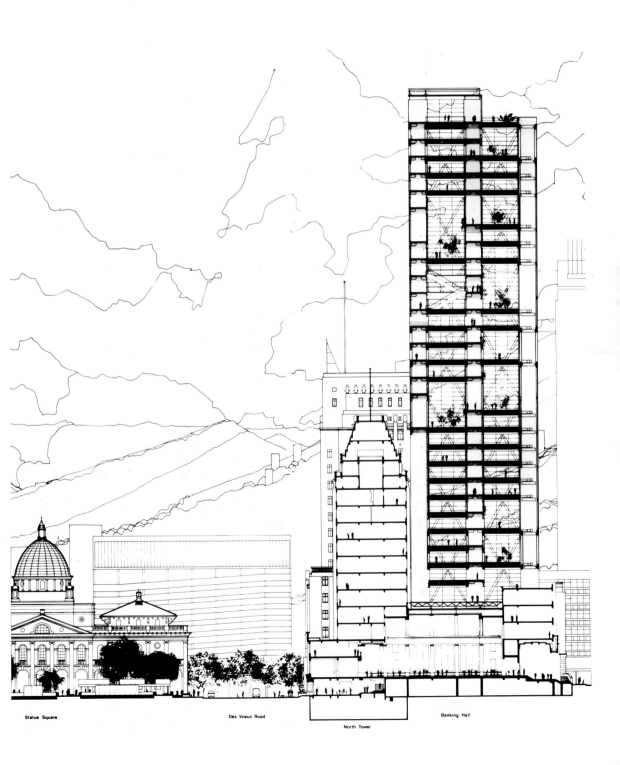

Statue Square

Des Voeux Road

North Tower

Banking Hall

[39] This decision did away with the concrete columns and the supply core, which were still incorporated in the first proposals.

[40] Norman Foster, 'Prologue', in: *Process Architecture*, No. 70, Sept. 1986, p. 7.

in the traditional sense. Secondly, the building would be conceived and produced as pre-fabricated elements, manufactured around the world and then shipped or airfreighted to the assembly point.[39] Thirdly, if industries outside the traditional sphere of the construction industry could offer a better performance then we would attempt to harness their skills and energies. Fourthly, we would actively collaborate with industry, using mock-ups and testing prototypes to anticipate, as far as possible, the eventual realities on site.'[40]

At the beginning of 1980 the team had developed a scheme that would be known, due to its V-shaped façade motif, as the 'chevron'. Numerous variants were developed before it was presented to the Bank's board in May. In both of the preferred schemes, the service shafts and modules were placed to the sides, outside the actual floor areas, which were defined by external steel columns. In the solution presented to the client, the façade is articulated by the contrast between the V-shaped cross-braces (set off in red) and the pattern of the cladding. These features offered much more freedom for the design of interior fixtures, particularly the possibility of omitting individual intermediate floors on certain levels. They also created new problems, however – for example, by requiring a considerably larger number of reinforcements between the supporting columns. And ultimately the chevron plans failed to meet the requirement for the setback of the eastern elevation specified by planning regulations in order to guarantee the supply of light to Bank Street, which runs nearby.[41]

[41] The architects had hoped for a change in this part of the building regulations while working on the scheme.

Despite the enthusiastic approval of the Chairman, the chevron plan was rejected by the Bank's board in May 1980. The Chinese members saw in it an unfortunate association with *fung-shui*, while the European members felt uncomfortable with the red colour of the structure, which had been chosen precisely with Chinese traditional symbolism in mind. In the opinion of the board, the architects had moved far, too far, from the neutral image of the first plan and the sobriety that should be displayed by a banking institution.

ON THE PATH TO THE 'FINAL SCHEME'

If the contractual obligations to complete the new building by July 1, 1985 were to be met, then the deadline for finalizing the scheme was January 1981. It was thus most important to find an acceptable solution as quickly as possible. Several monochrome models of July 1980 show alternatives that were considered after the decision of the Bank's board. One of them returns to the theme of the chevron plan, though with solid façades that were irreconcilable with the required setbacks on the east elevation. Another model solves this problem by stepping back the façade floor by floor. The idea is developed of several

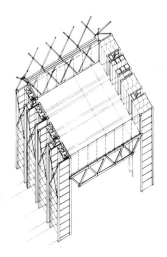

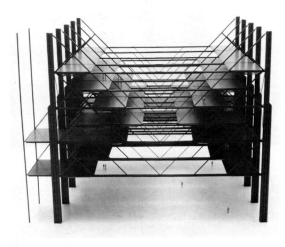

Further development of
the chevron plan. Spatial
simulation of the 'gull's
wing' ceiling.

staggered slabs, one behind another. These are deeper than in the chevron plans, and one can begin to distinguish suspended hanger-shaped constructions on the double main masts on the sides. Since none of the gigantic Andreas crosses that stiffened the construction were meant to be visible on the façade, intermediate floors on both sides of the central hollow had to be reinforced. This basic structure now evolved into the idea of a central atrium, and the architects returned to the double-height floors of the competition entry, whose space is dominated by the braces.

In the months to come, the scheme progressed to its final form. The architects modified the principle of the two hangers and combined them to form continuous trusses extending the full width – this was also a partial return to the earlier scheme. Reinforcement of the main masts provided adequate rigidity for each level and thus made it possible to reduce the number of braces on the elevations. The forms of the load-bearing beams were resolved: the Bank wanted them to be square in section, as an expression of stability and security, while Foster, also for aesthetic reasons, wanted circular cross-sections. Finally, the two parties agreed on circular columns and rectangular beams.

In a design process lasting more than two years the building underwent endless transformations, although the final scheme clearly has its roots in the very first ideas. The arrangement of space, which now displays clear contexts and hierarchies, was profoundly transformed. For example, the atrium, originally a subordinate space, had now become a virtual cathedral nave.

The studies for the main banking hall clearly show this metamorphosis: the principles remain the same, while the forms that they take continue to develop. An early series of drawings, dated August 26 and 27 with a modification of September 17, corresponds to the design phase with the hanger-shaped main construction. Despite the impression of transparency and monumentality, the space of the atrium is nothing out of the ordinary. The following series, dated in November, corresponds to the final scheme for the structure; here, strikingly, the hall is a space of exciting dynamism, where the horizontal open levels and the vertical nave complement each other in masterly fashion.

In 1981 the team produced a scheme to provide the pedestrian concourse running under the building with a floor of glass bricks, in order to integrate it into the concept of the atrium: huge mirrors were to reflect natural light into the floor beneath, housing the deposit vaults and the museum, which was still included at that stage. At night a 'crystalline glow' would have emerged from the basement of the

Model of the atrium.

Following double page: the completed building of the Hongkong and Shanghai Banking Corporation, 1979–1986.

building.[42] Doubts about the construction and maintenance costs, however, led to the rejection of this idea.

Also rejected was a detail of the interior furnishings of the offices which would have had rare visual force: a *faux plafond* in the form of a seagull's wing. This new type of ceiling evolved as a result of the suspended floor. Since the floor freed the ceiling from the weight of the air-conditioning ducts, the ceiling space could be used architecturally to diffuse the light. Alternating with noise-absorption panels, aluminium deflectors would reflect light to the workplaces. The 'gull's wing' configuration was tested with laser imitations and full-size models in modules of 1.2 to 2.4 m. Regrettably, work on this intermediate ceiling design was dropped in 1982, when new requirements of the Bank made necessary the introduction of a module grid of 1.2 m for all office furnishings.

In some cases the restrictions forced upon the team during the design stage proved to be constructive. The tricky problem of fire protection of the steel structure offers an eloquent example. Foster would have preferred to leave the steel of the load-bearing structure visible. The technical problems proved insoluble, however, and in the final design the steel is used merely in its classical role as the surface cladding. The perfecting of this cladding plays an important role precisely in the architectural fascination generated by the tower.

In 1986 Foster expressed his regret at the rejection of the glass floor of the pedestrian concourse, the hanging gardens, and the extravagant structure of the chevron plan. In a 1987 discussion he paid homage to this 'holistic and organic structural system'; it was, he said, 'like a bee's nest in which it is possible to create autonomous and very different internal spaces just by scratching a little, by digging a little with your finger. But even having been abandoned it had its value as one of the intermediate stages that are necessary in order to reach that clear simplicity, the result of long detours and many failed alternatives. Without them the building would not be what it is: 'Organic product of a site whose four sides are very different, indeed contradictory, and at the same time a rational object in which everything seems to be irrevocably at its only proper place: the urban front, the three-dimensional volume, the response to the urban-design specifications, the gradual transition from an open ground floor accessible to the public to floors above that become increasingly private, the logic of the supply and access systems.'

[42] Norman Foster, 'Hong Kong and Shanghai Banking Corporation Headquarters', *AD*, No. 51, March/April 1981, p. 26.

A skyscraper for the 21st century

Internal spaces: typical office, restaurant, and office area in double-height level.

The administrative headquarters of the Hongkong and Shanghai Banking Corporation is basically a huge office building with a total area of approximately 100 000 m². Despite its large dimensions, this this commission afforded Foster the unique opportunity to develop a new architecture for the service sector, down to the smallest detail. The creators of the building, clients and architects, jointly set themselves two main aims: maximum transparency and optimum flexibility.

TRANSPARENCY

The principle of transparency in fact encompasses two demands: an open view for everyone and, tendentiously, the perfect visibility of everyone by everyone. Providing all of the workplaces with outside views means in this case allowing all 3500 employees to enjoy a magnificent prospect – for the south-facing side of the tower looks out on the island's mountains, the Victoria Peak, and the Botanical Gardens, while the north side overlooks the bay, the harbour and the Chinese mainland. This approach meets the desire for comprehensive natural lighting – even in the 50 m² central areas of the standardized floors, which account for two-thirds of the total height of the building.

For the office landscape the client expressed the specific desire that each individual workplace should be visible, those of the principal employees included. The practicable solution was a rule that the view from each workplace should be no less than a third and no more than half of the building's depth.

Critics have noted that this implied a potential for visual 'control' that was in fact irreconcilable with the social standards of the architect. By way of contrast such critics cite the work of Hermann Hertzberger, especially his 1972 Centraal Beheer office complex in Appeldorn. Compared with this strategy of the 1970s, often invoked as exemplary, the spatial arrangement of the Hongkong Bank appears to be oriented to a single-tier work environment, lending itself to virtually inquisitorial control. But could one truly describe it as socially tolerable if the internal rooms of Centraal Beheer were to be jumbled together over 40 storeys? One cannot view the tower as a theoretical model for the solution of the problem of work control; on the contrary, it was created at a time when this problem had taken on a fundamentally different form. In an information age, the control function has largely passed from the organization of space to the electronics sector; now the organization of space can be used in more subtle ways, with the aim of motivating employees and furthering their identification with the company. In the case of the Hongkong Bank, it is not only the factual, but also the visual unification of the different

company sectors that conveys a positive image in which performance is linked with openness to the future.

FLEXIBILITY

From the first stages of design, the architects made an effort to create large continuous surfaces in the Hongkong Bank and to prevent them from being broken up by heavy elements. Almost all vertical elements of the load-bearing structure and of the circulation system and services were therefore integrated into the external walls, with the exception of the central escalators for local access and the masts that provide the primary suspension system of the structure. From the outset the internal organization of the tower was multifunctional, and there were no thoughts of any type of hierarchy, not even of a permanent overall form. With this brief, the only areas subject to preconditions were the entry halls, which necessarily had to be kept close to the ground.

Flexibility also includes the idea of the 'service module' as an autonomous unit. In the course of the design process these capsules increasingly assumed the form of service shafts that represented durability more than mutability: while their detachment from the interior space does make it possible to change them completely in their technology and their functions, they are fixed in place as units. Originally it was not only the service modules but entire office floors that were planned as replaceable. The floors were envisioned as steel constructions capable of complete disassembly, so that it would be possible not only to create an empty space (an atrium, for example), but to create a different atrium at every point. The finished building, however, used more conventional permanent concrete floor slabs in order to avoid the risk of vibration effects inherent in suspended intermediate floors. Flexibility is thus confined to the space between two intermediate floors and no longer extends to the entire fabric and internal space.[43] But because the internal space of every floor can be completely restructured, the clients' main aim – the option of comprehensive reorganization of all services – has been achieved.

In this bid for radical flexibility demonstrated by the first design phases the influence of Buckminster Fuller is recognizable, namely 'the idea of flexibility on a large scale, the unlimited application of technical means, the lightness of the structures and the capability of smooth adaptation to always new situations', as Kenneth Frampton puts it.[44] The Climatroffice[45] already presented the floors of the levels not just as surfaces, but as open three-dimensional structures in which the services could be freely arranged. The flexibility in the Hongkong Bank owes much to this radically different concept of floor slabs.

[43] Exceptions are the space of the atrium, which could be closed by intermediate floors, as well as the eastern façade, where the set-back in the built volume could be closed up in the event of a change in building laws, thus allowing additional useable area.

[44] Kenneth Frampton, 'Du néo-productivisme au post-modernisme', L'Architecture aujourd'hui, no. 213, February 1981, p. 3.

[45] Cf. p. 38

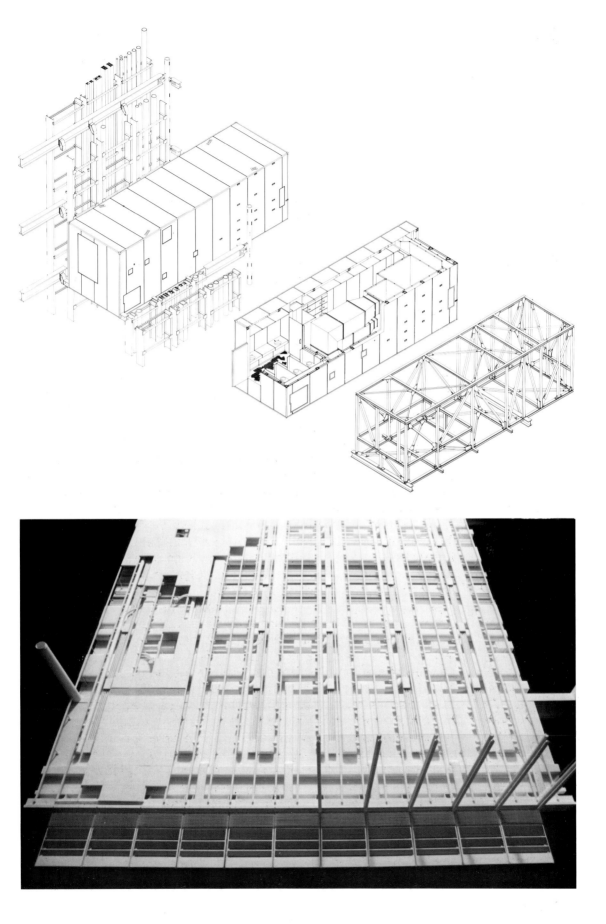

COMPONENT
SYSTEMS

On another level, flexibility is illustrated by the method of component manufacturing that the team perfected. The elements, most of which were produced especially for this project, were prefabricated in a large number of countries far from the actual construction site. In this way the architectural object is transformed into a highly organized complex of components, of systems, of 'apparatuses', as a theoretician of Russian production art, Nikolai Tarabukin, put it in the 1920s.[46]

[46] Nikolai Tarabukin, 'Le dernier tableau . . .' French edition, Paris, 1980.

An exceptional synthesis takes place here conceptually as well as with respect to materials. The intensive convergence of a variety of interests goes far beyond the old client–architect relationship; the users will be able to make fundamental changes in the space created here without further participation by the architect. It is no longer the architect and the user and the client as individuals whose interests determine the final form; instead, many negotiations and considerations create a system that is capable of reacting to supply and demand in use. The building becomes what is known in contemporary music as an 'open work'.

This wholeness is expressed by the clearly organized component catalogue and the user manual. In this case the user manual is the 'Interior Masterplan Report', which was presented to the client in December 1986. It is neither a technical description nor a set of instructions for maintenance of the various facilities, but rather a guide for ensuring maximum performance from the building, aesthetically as well as technically, for some of its instructions are aimed exclusively at spatial expression. The Masterplan is to a certain extent a record of this totality of modifiable systems, and through it the appearance of the building is determined.

ACCESS
STRATEGIES

One of the key problems of their skyscraper building type is that of access, both internally and from without. The architect writes: 'Given Hong Kong crowds it is probably impossible to calculate the magnitude of movement through the site, but it has been predicted that visitors to the building may exceed 20 000 a day, quite apart from the office population itself. The form of the building reflects the movement and density of use, with the greatest public footprint at the base, tapering to the least dense and most private areas at the top. Vertical travel is by a combination of high speed lifts and escalators through a sequence of varied spaces.'[47] The lifts are not the quickest that have been developed, but one can travel in them from the ground floor to the top in 27 seconds.[48] Above the entry halls they stop only on the four double-height floors which divide up the tower visually into five horizontal zones. The central escalators, as local access paths, connect

[47] Norman Foster, 'Hong Kong Banking Corporation Headquarters', AD, No. 51, March/April 1981, p. 26.

[48] Data provided by Ray Guy in a lecture in Glasgow on January 13, 1986.

these spaces to the intermediate floors. The movement is leisurely, and one has the chance to enjoy the view.

This mixed system has proven exceptionally effective. Not only does it offer the advantages that one usually finds only in low buildings – and its resemblance to Willis Faber & Dumas is obvious – it also enriches the architectural experience with a variety of spaces seen in constant motion. As with towers in a narrower sense, such as the Eiffel Tower, 'The visitor moves upwards vertically, horizontally and at a number of different angles. In Foster's building he will normally travel up by both lift and escalator, travelling through double-height spaces rich with water, air, light, foliage and cafes.'[49] The dimension of movement combines with other aspects of the building, such as transparency. The result is a new type of *promenade architecturale* that speaks to all the senses. At the same time it presents a hierarchy of spaces according to their accessibility, completing the differentiation between public, semi-public and private areas. In its sensitivity to such symbolism – this word to be understood in its psychological and not its post-modern sense – Foster's concept of space is much closer to the Eastern understanding than the Western.

The biggest task in the new approach to this differentiation is, of course, the transition between outside and inside, on the urban design scale as well as in the scale of the building.

49 Jonathan Glancey, 'Hong Kong Bank', *The Architectural Review*, No. 1011, May 1981.

STEPS OF RAPPROCHE-MENT

The building should really be approached by boat, in the traditional manner of arrival in Hong Kong. At first the tower rises in front of the massive rock formations of the island; then, as one draws closer, it dominates the great public space, Statue Square, at its foot. One recognizes the high entrance hall that is designed as a pedestrian concourse; the first floor above it is twice the height of the next one and mediates between this public domain and the areas above. The entry plaza of the ground floor, between the gigantic load-bearing masts, is effectively a continuation of the pedestrian zone of Statue Square and connects it with Queen's Road behind, Hong Kong's most affluent street and also one of its oldest traffic arteries. This north–south passage has not only a practical function but also a deeply symbolic one: to the north is the harbour, Kowloon and the Chinese mainland, to the south the colonial centre. The tower had to be open to both sides. Its central atrium, the different configurations of the north and south façades, as well as the broad opening of the pedestrian route are considered responses to this fact. The old headquarters of the Bank, built on the same site in 1886, had consisted literally of two different, mutually complementary parts: a colonial building on one side and a classical European building on the other.

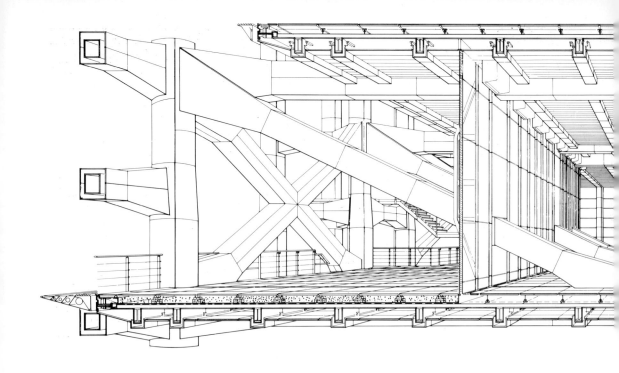

Isometric perspective:
load-bearing structure
in a double-height level.

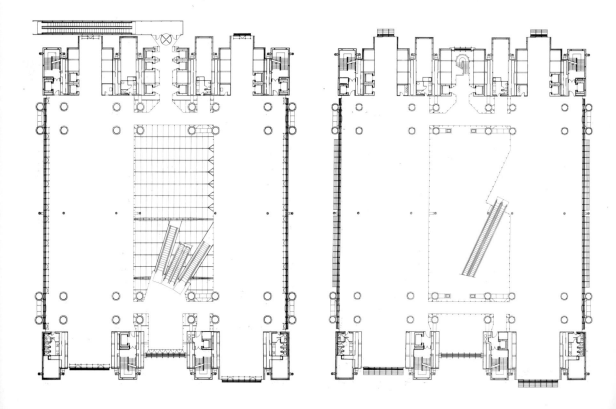

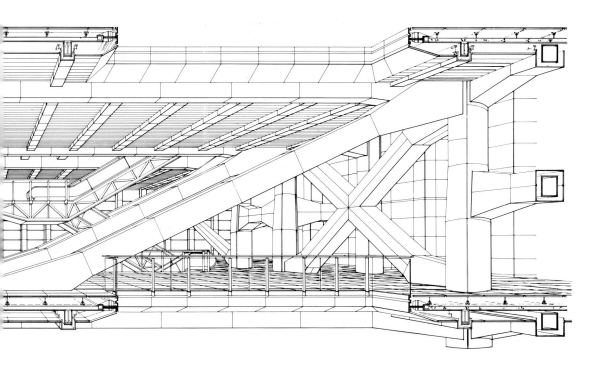

Floor plans: public
banking hall and
secondary banking floor,
typical atrium floor,
typical upper floor.

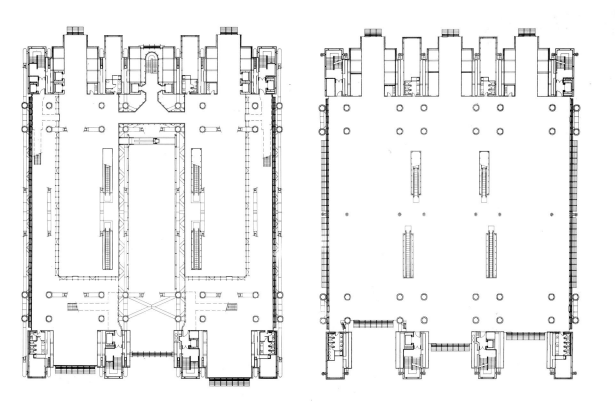

Internal access: East–
West section, schematic
sketch of the circulation
system with escalators
and lifts.

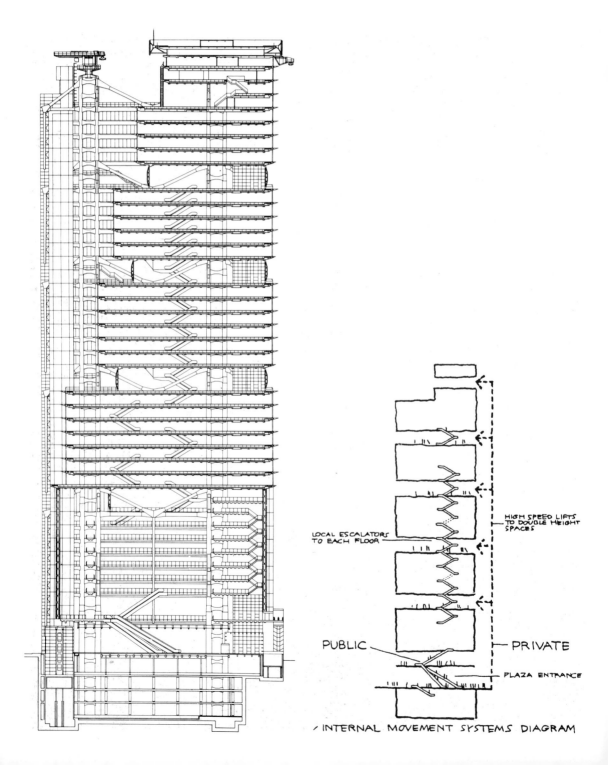

HIGH SPEED LIFTS
TO DOUBLE HEIGHT
SPACES

LOCAL ESCALATORS
TO EACH FLOOR

PUBLIC

PRIVATE

PLAZA ENTRANCE

INTERNAL MOVEMENT SYSTEMS DIAGRAM

Sketch for the 'sunscoop'.

View upwards from the ground floor through the glass ceiling into the atrium.

[50] Even the floor of the entrance hall was designed to be transparent; it was to be built of glass bricks and to be lit from the basement. This feature was not included in the built version, however.

[51] The external reflector, guided by a computer-controlled mechanism, follows precisely the sun's position on the horizon from day to day, though not its course from east to west.

Two monumental escalators freely arranged on the plaza lead up to the hall 12 m above the ground with its ten-storey atrium. The escalators pass through a 1000 m² membrane of clear glass, which is the product of a long search for a light, transparent structure that would insulate the atrium from below without blocking the view from the ground floor hall.[50] From the many alternatives, such as space frames, tension structures, or arches, a rigid steel-and-glass catenary form on the principle of a rope bridge was finally chosen. It is absolutely regular in order to avoid any visual confusion, and the fineness of its structure makes it one of the most successful parts of the building.

The atrium, the first internal space one encounters, is the most impressive space in the building. It rises ten stories to a height of 49.8 m above the floor of the plaza. From a point at middle height, the floors suspended above each other seem to float in space; one can look through the entire depth of the building and beyond, out into the city. But one's eyes are involuntarily drawn to the top floor, Level 11, in the centre of which is the gigantic internal reflector of the 'sunscoop'. A second reflector is located outside on the south façade; this collects the sunlight and directs it horizontally over 25 m to the concave internal canopy, which reflects it vertically into the space of the atrium, all the way down to the ground floor.[51] Thus, the first 11 floors of the building are bathed in a remarkable, exhilarating brightness; and yet this system was actually conceived as an architectural means of supplying light and visually integrating the ground floor into the atrium. Structurally the 'sunscoop' is probably the most spectacular element of the tower.

Foster's handling of the tension between the public and the private accounts for much of the originality of his work. As one approaches the building from the city, the sequence of square, plaza and atrium represents the first phase of transition from public to less public spaces. In the banking halls the architect has even succeeded in overcoming the physical barrier of the cashiers' windows, which normally separate the public from the bank's employees. However, this sequence proved impossible to maintain consistently, for the other areas of the tower are relatively independent of the banking halls, not only functionally but also spatially. Employees can reach the principal floors directly via separate lifts from small glazed bays in the plaza, behind the mighty load-bearing masts.

In the areas above the atrium, local access by escalators enables the creation of a number of 'villages in the sky', as Foster calls them – each one of which, like the old villages on the southern coast of China, has its boundaries, its own paths, its special character. One

might suggest that the formation of vertical zones represents a new variant of the deep floor plan. These stacks do not represent an attempt to produce a very precise correspondence between spatial structure and function, even if the division into five large zones is visible on the façade: first, the area for current banking transactions, above it the data service, then the international services, general administration, and the Chairman's office at the top. In fact, the formation of 'villages' is designed to reinforce the employees' sense of community.

A NEW TYPE OF HIGH-RISE

With this concept of semi-public areas the Hongkong Bank overcomes the conventional high-rise structures of strict divisions, isolated entrance halls and blind corridors.

Foster's building displays the three zones of the classic skyscraper: the base, extended middle section, and clear conclusion at the top, just as defined by Louis Sullivan. Post-modernism has also returned to this convention, but with Foster it derives from an analysis of human relationships and has nothing in common with a pure play of forms. A similar approach is shown in his high-rise design for the Humana Corporation in Louisville, USA, created in 1982, while the Bank was under construction. Here as well there is a large, open atrium connected to a neighbouring art centre, while the top of the tower is formed by an expressive antenna mast.

The emphasis on the vertical is certainly not restricted to the external structure, but is felt on many different levels. The clearly perceptible movements of rise and fall in all areas of the tower play a large role. As Alain Pélissier writes, it is 'true celestial architecture. The rooms at the very top, for the VIPs, are oriented downward . . . From this dominant point the entire city offers itself up to observation . . . Visual immersion is omnipresent: in the distribution of the double-height intermediate halls . . . but also in the standard floors, where the work areas hover over the city . . . These unusual interior spaces make the tower a terminus and high point. No other building in the history of skyscrapers relates its spaces to the vertical as dramatically . . .'[52] Pélissier also notes how the form of the smooth, towering columns, the hanging glass ceiling, and the shimmering of the metal evoke impressions of frictionless gliding which are echoed in the actual movement of the escalators and in the flood of light. The result is a world of subtle but also powerful refinement, animated by varying contrasts between slender, simple, almost femininely gentle forms and others whose effect is rougher, more brutal and masculine.

Chris Abel finds a different accent in the double-height floors: 'No matter what, it is impossible to shake off the feeling that one has

[52] Alan Pélissier, 'Foster à Hong Kong. Les nouvelles dimensions de l'espace-tour', in: *Techniques et Architecture*, No. 372, July 1987, pp 113 and 117.

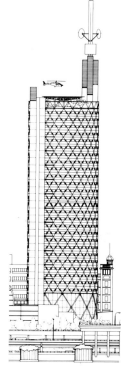

stumbled into some outsize converted attic, where people and furniture have to make the best of what room they can find between the rafters.'[53] And in fact the atmosphere of the restaurant, with its tuxedo-clad waiters working around the expansive escalators, has something undeniably surreal about it. Who would have dreamed that the interior of a skyscraper might awaken memories of attics from childhood days, precisely as the philosopher, Gaston Bachelard, wished?[54] The large structural elements and service installations on top of the building completely dominate the elegant skin. Here the interplay between vision and construction create an astonishing effect: VIP suites, tai-pan apartments, maintenance cranes and a helicopter landing pad: what a film set! And those who, here in this detached, armoured pavilion high up in the sky, detect a lack of equilibrium between the gigantic construction and the delicacy of the interior, should refer back to the atrium, where the contradictions of this building, which conjures up King Kong one moment and Madame Butterfly the next, blend in a way as astonishing as it is moving.

[53] Chris Abel, 'A Building for the Pacific Century', in *The Architectural Review*, No. 1070, April 1986, p. 58.

[54] Gaston Bachelard, *La poétique de l'espace*, Paris 1957.

Urban design dialogue

BBC Radio Headquarters, London, 1982–85: sketches on the historical development of the urban design situation, simulation of the building in context (view from the north). Site plan: Portland Place to the north, Oxford Street to the south, the BBC building between Cavendish Square and All Souls Church.

THE PROJECT FOR THE BBC

55 The BBC is a microcosm of British culture; Foster spoke of an "assembly of hostile tribes".

56 The diagonal cross-section through the orthogonal system produces a simple triangular figure with side proportions of 3:4:5.

In the 1980s, Norman Foster also worked for the first time on several projects whose challenges and charm derive primarily from their urban context. The Radio Headquarters for the BBC in London and the Médiathèque in Nîmes were both designed for unusually sensitive inner-city sites constrained by their proximity to important historical buildings, but even more strongly by their prominent situation in the urban fabric. By contrast, the King's Cross Redevelopment project in London demanded a comprehensive new urban design scheme for its 52 ha area. Foster's designs for these projects are characteristic of his attitude toward the city, and they demonstrate that it is in this area that he has moved the farthest from the masters of modernism.

The office and studio building designed for the BBC in the heart of London faced two challenging tasks: it had to meet the requirements of an extremely diverse programme and at the same time integrate itself into an exceptionally rich urban environment. The BBC expected above all an analysis of and a strategy for a project that is tailored to the organization of a radio broadcasting service with its various departments: music, theatre, news, school programmes and, of course, administrative facilities, archives, etc.[55] The old building is spatially and acoustically no longer adequate. In his scheme Foster retains this building to provide ancillary accommodation beside his new building on an adjacent site belonging to the BBC. The site is on the double bend where Portland Place joins Upper Regent Street, opposite All Souls Church. It is occupied by the Langham Hotel, a listed historical landmark, a bulky and visually awkward nineteenth century building; this was to be replaced by a building that would consciously mediate between the calm atmosphere of Portland Place to the north and busy Oxford Street to the south.

Many variations were explored; the scheme finally chosen was based on an axis lying diagonal to the street grid[56] connecting Cavendish Square to the rear of the site with All Souls, and extending farther to the British Telecom Tower some 700 m away. On the ground floor this axis is defined by a publicly accessible atrium that dissects the building from corner to corner. It allows passers-by to participate in the feverish activity of this public institution, and, conversely, the great glass façade affords a beautiful view of the old church from inside. On the other elevations, façades of stone and opaque glass precisely follow the course of the streets. Its height develops along the diagonal axis, beginning with a low, sedate elevation on Cavendish Square and reaching its highest point toward Regent Street. Here other important urban design references are developed: the pinnacle of the atrium echoes the church across the street; a projecting block

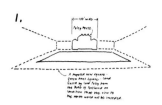

1.

IN THE BEGINNING........
CAVENDISH SQUARE 1717 ON
FOLEY HOUSE 1758

2

AN ARCHITECTURAL STAGE SET · STATIC ·

FRAMING COUNTRYSIDE TO THE NORTH &

CLOSING VISTA OF FOLEY HOUSE TO SOUTH

ADAM BROTHERS 1778

3

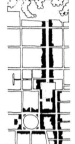

THE DYNAMIC OF A NEW PROCESSIONAL ROUTE

NASH · 1812 - 21

4

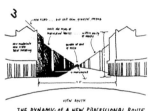

VIEW SOUTH

THE LANGHAM 1864

5

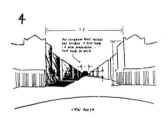

VIEW SOUTH

1920's TO NOW

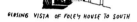

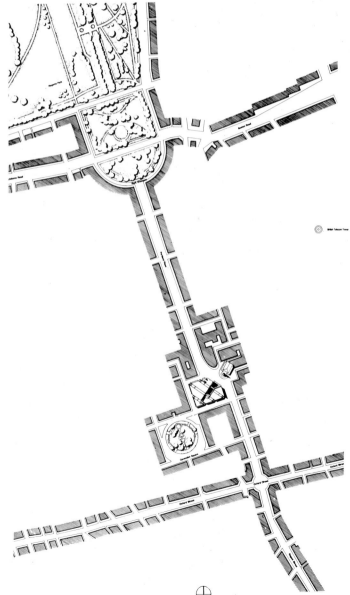

0   50   100   150M

BBC Radio Headquarters. The main axis is developed as an atrium.

Top: the BBC Radio Headquarters with adjacent All Souls Church. Bottom: the Médiathèque in Nîmes with the neighbouring ancient temple (model of the implemented scheme).

corresponds to the façade of Broadcasting House, the existing BBC building; and the lift towers above the main entrance provide punctuation at the southern end of Portland Place.

The building for the BBC is undoubtedly one of Foster's most complex and most successful designs, and yet it must also join the long rank of unsuccessful projects. After a design process beginning in 1982 and lasting several years, the scheme was finally dropped by the BBC when George Howard, the director who had been responsible, left the company and other managers decided to acquire a site in West London.

THE CARRÉ D'ART IN NÎMES

The southern French city of Nîmes, on the western edge of Provence, boasts precious ruins from the ancient past, among them the Maison Carrée, the best preserved temple in all the territories that once belonged to the Roman Empire. The mayor wanted to find an architectural 'star' for construction of a médiathèque and contemporary art centre facing the Maison Carrée. Of the twelve prestigious names recommended to him, four were invited to submit designs. The first prize was won in 1984 by the rather sober contribution of Norman Foster, whose design most clearly reflected the urban surroundings and the affluent neighbourhood. The main challenge was in fact posed by the Maison Carrée.

On the site of a theatre destroyed by fire in 1952, Foster designed a rectangle whose eastern façade, which faces the temple, is composed of three elements: an asymmetrically positioned open stairway and a front hall of reduced height under a deep projecting canopy supported by two slender columns, representing essentially a modern answer to the temple portico. The projecting canopy, whose proportions carefully reflect those of the temple, closes off one of the principal visual axes, that of the main avenue. Moreover, the scheme harmonizes with the western façade and the glass-roofed courtyard, which is accessed from a corner in order to connect it visually with the Place Carrée.

The building as it was completed at the beginning of the 1990s was the result of a long planning process in which several versions of the project were proposed for political, strategic and architectural reasons. In the original competition entry, the visually heavy projecting canopy overhung the entrance plinth and the steps like a gigantic visor. The huge façade walls were to serve as a projection screen for video art, and to be hung with flags the rest of the time. The plinth could also serve as a stage, while the space between the Maison Carrée and Médiathèque would accommodate spectators or provide a venue for other events, such as open-air exhibitions. Circulation

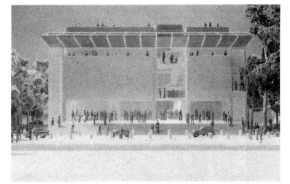

within the building was by ramps suspended in the atrium space, and the exhibition spaces were lit by wells that channelled the light onto funnel-shaped reflectors. In one phase, responding to a campaign for the preservation of the old theatre of 1803, an attempt was made to integrate a preserved colonnade into the building, but this would have obstructed the entrance. All these variations employed a concrete structure and façades of stainless steel, bronze, and local stone.

The adaptations in the course of the design process essentially affect the façades, particularly the east façade, in order to correspond to the asymmetrically positioned atrium. Overall the building assumes a lighter form as more glass is introduced to the façades and the floor plan becomes more regular. The internal organization is simple: service and storage spaces are located in the basement; the Média-thèque (with various libraries as well as shops) is located on the elevated ground floor; the top two floors are occupied by the art gallery. To illuminate the top floor the architect employs a solution similar to that of the Sainsbury Centre in Norwich. Thus, the competition entry, whose form is determined primarily by the constraints of urban design, gradually assumes the traits and characteristics of Foster's architecture.

In both projects – the radio headquarters and the Carré d'Art – one can observe a specific dialogue between the environment and the architectural scheme. The buildings are carefully tailored to the site not only in their external forms, but their public character is also evident in the interior, which is usually treated independently. The site determines the structure of the building, providing the main axis and the spatial organization with meaning and significance, whether it be the gigantic complex in London or the jewel in Provence.

In these commissions the architect performed his analysis primarily by sketches. During planning for the British Rail site at London's King's Cross station, however, he made greater use of computers, as a reaction to the larger dimensions of the project and above all to the significantly greater scope for decision-making he was granted.

KING'S CROSS REDEVELOP- MENT

57 Foster has always been an opponent of such urban proliferation; here he stands in the modernist tradition of Le Corbusier, a posture that remains alien to the Anglo-Saxon countries.

The expansion of the city into surrounding agricultural land is no longer regarded – apart from the creation of 'new towns' on green field sites – as the only way of urban development.[57] For years now an alternative school of thought has been gaining support, refocussing attention on the old, often neglected urban centres, or on the suburbs created by the industrial development of the nineteenth and first half of the twentieth centuries. These are often in very bad condition, marked by vast 'industrial wastelands' which city residents will drive around without ever noticing. It was inevitable that Foster would one

King's Cross
Redevelopment, London,
at planning stage since
1987. First urban design
plan.

day be confronted by the regeneration of just such a large neglected area. The work on the vicinity of King's Cross railway station in London, begun in 1987, is Foster's first project of this type.

To the north of King's Cross and St Pancras stations, which form one of the most important transport interchanges in London, British Rail owns a huge property with old railway and industrial buildings, of roughly 52 ha. In their urban design planning, Foster Associates refer back to pre-modern examples for their design of the urban image, as well as to striking features such as the Circus in Bath and Regent's Park in London. An analysis will show how Foster thus indirectly responds to Prince Charles's criticism of modern architecture from the beginning of the 1980s and to his demand for a return to the solutions of the past as a remedy for the defects of modernism, in urban planning as well as architecture.

The first schemes already show a clear linkage of the three essential components: a large vaulted glass roof between the two existing train stations; a built-up area organized according to the traditional street plan; and inside this the third most important element of the physical development plan: an elliptical park with an area of 2.5 ha.

The large glazed vault was made necessary by the anticipated influx of travellers arriving from the continent via the Channel Tunnel: it would be a new gateway to England. In its proximity to two brilliant examples of iron architecture, Foster's selection of one of his favourite themes, the glass vault, takes on typological significance. In an initial scheme Foster connects the existing vaults of the two railway stations with a wedge-shaped vault that later resolves into an assembly of individual shells, also in the shape of wedges. It maintains a respectful distance from the old buildings. Foster decided in favour of transparency, and in fact there is not a single façade in the new building[58] that would compete with those of King's Cross and St Pancras: the glass curtain wall does not actually close off the building, but rather allows it to extend its sense of movement into the square at the front.

The built-up area consists of a belt of buildings connected to the two stations. The first schemes contain alternatives to this continuous peripheral development which provide for a regular interruption of the building belt and thus open up the development more to the central park. The regular, elliptical form of the park,[59] accentuated by a wreath of plane trees, gives it an immediate sense of unity despite extremely diverse landscaping.

The first urban design models are distinguished by a clarity that emphasizes a comprehensive idea. They have a clear aim: to create a balance between profit and public well-being, between the

[58] It is significant that Foster provides the stations with new vaulting rather than with new façades. Throughout his work he has preferred transparent skins to traditional façades.

[59] Large parts of the 250 x 275 m park are the work of Edouard Hutchinson, who was hired as the landscape architect.

King's Cross. Designs for the new station between King's Cross Station and St. Pancras Station. Drawing of the first scheme. Model of the revised scheme, with the triangular roof broken up into nine trigonometric shells.

demands of the property business and collective, social benefit. This aim is in contrast to urban schemes implemented in other parts of London, plans in which the dominant factor is clearly maximum profit for the developer. Particularly remarkable is the manifestation of this balance in the actual design drawings, almost in the geometry of the lines. Like nowhere else, Foster has returned here to a classic theme of British architectural history. Though clearly disinterested in mere nostalgic repetition of past architectural styles – despite his interests in such things as historical *brises-soleil*, for the gentle acquisition of energy in the tropics, or the beauty of Japanese houses – Foster here seems to have returned to the baroque inclination toward the sublime and the grand gesture. But his ideas go beyond this: the grand gesture is not their sole aim. For him the organization of the belt of buildings around the open park opens up numerous design possibilities.

The studies began by examining density, height, the view into the park, and especially the streets, whose configuration is seen as vital for the proper functioning of the city: correctly arranged streets prevent the formation of ghettos by guaranteeing a more or less uniform density of traffic movements, of pedestrians in particular. Foster was able to call on the specialist knowledge of a team[60] that has developed a method of analysis called 'spatial syntax', which allows the diverse implications of a scheme to be assessed with the assistance of a computer.

[60] A research group of University College in London headed by Bill Hillier, lecturer at the Bartlett School.

The programme analyses all the data in a certain zone and its adjacent areas. It provides information about the density of traffic flow for each street of the network projected by the scheme. The computer depicts the network as a collection of lines: the analysis gives each line a weighting in relation to the adjacent lines, taking into account the pattern of movements that lead from one line to another, and the frequency with which each line participates in the most direct movements between the lines. The weightings are colour-coded: white has the greatest weight and expresses a high degree of integration of the line into the entire area; here there is a high volume of simple movement. Green, by contrast, shows a high degree of isolation: the path is rarely frequented and is part of a complex circulation system. Orange indicates streets of moderate movement density. Well-structured urban zones make maximum use of the integrating (white) lines to connect the core of the area both to the large-scale urban network and to the smaller streets within the district, thus guaranteeing a mixture of quiet and busy streets.

The computer analyses enable the formulation of rules; they show that a development will be best served by a coherent network of

white lines. These lines should be as long and straight as possible, they should allow long views and clear connections between distant points. For the area to function as a whole, these lines must cover it comprehensively; thus, they will lead to a mixture of colours on all parts of the site plan. Their number must be restricted, however, for an excess of white lines in any area would mean that that area dominates the others, which would result in a strong concentration of only local paths elsewhere.

With the help of analyses of this type, and following the rules derived from them, later versions of the scheme increasingly acquired profile and context, especially with better definition of housing blocks and streets along which the buildings are arranged. The version of May 1988 specifically improves the housing blocks on the northern tip, which previously stood in isolation, by introducing a long street that crosses the area from northwest to southeast, preventing the creation of an office ghetto by assigning a prominence to the street and path network.

The most recent version of the scheme modifies the entire site plan, reorganizing it while retaining its essential components. The earlier arrangement of the building complexes bordering the park and the street network radiating from it prevented a direct connection with the two stations. The new plan avoids this isolation by redefining the built fabric, the street routing and the visual axes, particularly between the park and stations, and by creating a more clearly shaped centre in the north.

The streets crossing through the development now open out into the two stations. One main street forms the boundary of the park on the west, but is separated from it by several rows of trees. They form a long promenade, interrupted only by the canal crossing. The park assumes a more public character, where before it was a more secluded square for those who lived around it. Its oval form is 'distorted'[61] to align it with the stations, but probably also to allow the perimeter configuration to shape itself to the infrastructure of the railway lines. Thus the texture of the crucial area is structured more effectively, and it no longer appears as a vaguely defined no-man's land, representing instead a transition to the city and simultaneously a definition of the park.

The horseshoe-shaped belt of buildings has been transformed into two arcs that spread out from the stations, circumscribing the almond shape of the park and intersecting at its north end. Giving emphasis to this point is a service area with two office towers that assume important urban design functions: they create an interesting skyline, while cushioning the resulting jump in scale with their differentiated

[61] Foster: "The requested oval form never satisfied us because it remained abstract. It did have some relation to the primary elements of the project, but it was awkward".

volumes; transparent façades allow the passer-by to glimpse the activities within them.

The entire area is now organically organized and integrated more closely into the city, whose main streets are naturally picked up and continued. There is emphasis on open spaces and water, which are used as precisely defined structuring elements. Foster creates the public domain primarily with spaces that are to be experienced with built masses.[62] It was particularly for this reason that the team devoted so much time to the planning of the street network,[63] the type of greenery and the proper scale of the strategically important areas, and it was for this reason also that so much value was placed on the mixture of urban functions, traffic flow and means of transport.[64] Foster proposed encouraging street cafés because they would create 'a type of semi-public, more organic space'.

Compared with the first proposals, the new station roof has diminished in volume. Its form and position are now determined by the two streets that run beside the old station buildings. The simple geometric vault has been divided into individual shells whose form recalls an African mask or the umbrella-like roofs designed by Hector Guimard for the entrances to the Paris metro. Foster writes: '... the need to create "a" train station both operationally and symbolically required a unifying element with a clear statement of entrance.'

The basic elements of the large park have also been refined: its three sections are more clearly formed, a paved square to the north provides a transition to the office towers, the gas holders are emphasized as an important feature, the clusters of trees are structured differently. Above all the treatment of the water surfaces shows Foster's understanding of the relationships between natural and architectural elements.

An illustration he uses is of a mid-nineteenth century granary building by Cubitt.[65] His approach is not simply sensitivity to the building itself, but also rediscovering its original setting. The granary originally related to a water basin, creating a different kind of water, which he calls 'hard' as opposed to the 'softer' water which makes its way south to the terminal. There is thus much more to landscaping than hard brick edges.

The park has thus lost its initial autonomy and, freed of all that is formalistic, it forms an integral part of the overall structure of the area.

[62] Foster does not want to introduce a unified language of forms, but proposes involving various well-known architects such as Raphael Moneo, Jean Nouvel, Jean-Michel Willmotte, and others.

[63] One of the streets picks up the proportions of Regent Street.

[64] Instead of underground transport, a streetcar is suggested, because it is "more similar to the human being".

[65] Lecture at the RIBA, 1989.

King's Cross. The revised
urban design scheme
with modifications to the
park and its canal, the
positioning of the station,
the traffic routes, and the
surrounding buildings. To
the north (left): the
service area with two
office towers.

Entrance of the Renault
Distribution Centre. Link
bridge and pedestrian
ramp between the two
buildings in the IBM
technology park in
Greenford.

Following double pages: On the ground floor of the Hongkong Bank. Escalators lead from the pedestrian concourse up to the atrium.

Façade of the Hongkong Bank, view down into a lift shaft.

A new glass stairwell ascends up between the old buildings of the Royal Academy to the Sackler Galleries.

Front of the Sainsbury
Centre,
skylight in Stansted
Airport,
roof of the swimming pool
in Century Tower.

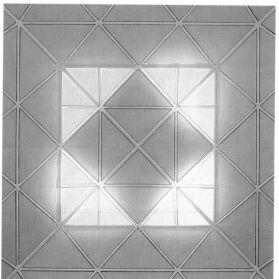

The town is reflected in
the façade of the Willis
Faber & Dumas
building.

Stansted Airport at twilight. The Hongkong Bank and Sainsbury Centre by night.

New projects

Stansted Airport, designed between 1981 and 1986 and opened in March 1991, is Foster Associates' outstanding achievement of the end of the decade. The third London airport is designed entirely around the passenger's route to the aeroplane. Most passengers arrive by train in the underground station; from there they progress to the full-length concourse and finally take a small train to the boarding satellite. The guiding idea was to make the aircraft visible from the main building from the moment the travellers arrive. The airy height of the hall that enables this[66] and the extremely simple organization of space allow the traveller to find his way around easily, particularly since the façades consist largely of translucent glass, thus directing one's gaze toward the runways.

66 The technical rationale for the high ceiling is its function as an exhaust zone for smoke in case of fires.

The first consideration for the scheme was not the technical problem presented by construction of the 32 000 m² hall, but rather the effect on people, the desire to give passengers a feeling of security, to take the drama out of travel. Instead of seeking the spectacular effect of an impressive structure as other new airport projects attempt to do (such as Meinhard von Gerkan's plans for the airports in Hamburg and Stuttgart), Foster seeks calm and equilibrium. For this reason the ceiling is treated as a dominant visual element, as a large, flowing, airy and glowing surface. The waves of the vaulted ceiling recall the Renault building, but the surface is both clearer and more sophisticated in structure than in Swindon. While the Renault building is a complicated technical wonder that even engineers can understand only with difficulty, the construction of Stansted is of a simplicity that evokes the great buildings of the nineteenth century. As in Swindon, the floor plan is based on a quadratic module, here with sides 36 meters square; the grid's supporting structure is in the form of tree-shaped columns that branch upward to the ceiling. The small number of columns in proportion to the ceiling area increases the impression of lightness. These 'trees', which look like oversized pieces of furniture from the Foster series, combine roof element, supporting structure and service unit in one.

The integration of service pods between the four very short columns of the 'trees' visually plays down their structural function, frees space, and emphasizes horizontality. Since Reliance Controls, Foster is always finding new ways of integrating service systems; here he fits them inside the structure, so that the beauty of the wide space is maintained.

One hears echoes of the architecture of Frei Otto or Pier Luigi Nervi, but above all Stansted recalls the American innovators of the

[67] Lecture to the RIBA, 1983.

1950s: Eero Saarinen, whose Dulles Airport in Philadelphia is a lesson in powerful simplicity, and Louis Kahn, whose treatment of light increasingly attracted Foster's interest.[67] Just as in their work, the light in Stansted is filtered and modulated. Each reflective ceiling dome has four rooflights in the centre, with panels suspended beneath them to prevent glare from sunlight. During the day these panels diffuse daylight and reflect it back onto the vaulting, while at night they reflect the beam of the spotlights and partially conceal the darkness of the sky.[68]

[68] The lighting system is the work of Danielle and Claude Engle.

Reflected light also plays an important role in the other parts of the building, for example in the underground station, where warm, orange light floods the concrete walls, in contrast to the clear colour scheme (various shades of white) in the concourse above.

To preserve the visual unity of the concourse, Foster has applied only a limited vocabulary of materials and colours and restricted the height of internal features to 3.75 m. The selection of colours is crucial for the atmosphere of lightness. As in most of Foster's works from the end of the 1980s, white predominates; the floor is a large expanse of pale granite; there are several touches of grey and the silvery shimmer of stainless steel; the only bright colours are the blue of the seats and the yellow of the direction signs.

Once again the project is distinguished by technical creativity – for example, in its solution to rainwater drainage from the huge, 40 000 m² roof surface. The team chose a siphonic system of a type widely used in Russia and Finland, in which the rainwater stands in the downpipes, rather than spiralling down around a central air current. The result is that with the comprehensive system of horizontal gutters the system requires an unusually low number of downpipes that were easy to integrate into the roof.

CONVERSION OF THE SACKLER GALLERIES

[69] One of the most enjoyable tasks of this project was the restoration of Norman Shaw's magnificent nineteenth-century stairway.

The Sackler Galleries, opened in June 1991 by Queen Elizabeth II, are the product of the difficult and complicated conversion of Burlington House, the home of the Royal Academy of Arts in London.[69] Use of the exhibition halls on the top floor of the building, known before as the Diploma Galleries, had been restricted because they were not easily accessible and no longer met the technical requirements of modern exhibitions. In the new scheme they were to be made accessible from two sides: directly from the main building and through a passage from the rear building, which also contains galleries. The two buildings are separated by a courtyard only a few metres wide. Here Foster designed a new stairwell and a lift whose glass housing presents a vivid contrast to the old, previously hidden

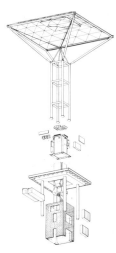

Terminal of Stansted Airport near London, 1981–91. Check-in area on concourse level, luggage sorting system in undercroft, detail of frame connection, exploded drawing of a structural 'tree'.

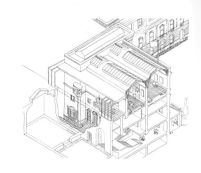

façades of the classical main building of 1660 and the newer Victorian building. The new galleries are top lit by an ingenious system that optimally combines natural and artificial light. The most impressive space is the new vestibule on the level of the galleries above the courtyard. Its white glass walls and partially glazed floor allow light to spill into the lower courtyard. The parapet of the Victorian building serves as a stand to exhibit sculptures, among which is the most valuable piece of the Royal Academy collection, a sculpture by Michelangelo.

The Crescent Wing, opened in 1991, is an extension of the Sainsbury Centre. It contains a gallery for sensitive artworks, which can also be used as a conference hall. It also houses the Reserve Collection Display, where the exhibits are preserved in glass cases, thus making the pieces that are not on display in the main gallery equally accessible to students and researchers. Conservation facilities are also located in the extension, with an excellent laboratory, which combines extreme functionality with great elegance in the best modern tradition. Finally, there are offices: these receive indirect light through a glass wall, which can be opened by swivelling it out into the long, curving corridor that gives the largely subterranean building its name.

EXTENSION OF THE SAINSBURY CENTRE, NORWICH

This form of ground plan is characteristic of the architect's newly awakened interest in existing forms. For even if several earlier projects already displayed such interest – such as Willis Faber & Dumas, several projects inspired by Fuller, or, more recently, a ring-shaped hotel design for the Holiday Inn group over a highway in The Hague (1987) – these geometries crop up much more frequently in schemes from the beginning of the 1990s. Concave or convex curves, in plan or in elevation – all possibilities are tested. This is a significant departure from earlier projects, whose formal simplicity came from the rectangle, the square and the angular grid. After the cylindrical Humana Tower, Foster uses three- to four-storey horizontal cylinder slices in the project for the Law Faculty at Cambridge University. The Shinagawa Project on Tokyo Harbour has the same profile in reverse, concave form – as, incidentally, does the swimming pool of Century Tower.

Other projects deviate from the simple form with compositions that differ from 'early Foster': examples of these include the Telecommunications Tower in Barcelona, design of which was begun in 1988, and a combined office, commercial and apartment building for Commerzbank in Frankfurt.

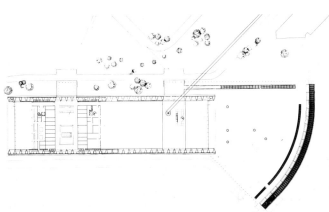

Crescent Wing, extension
of Sainsbury Centre,
Norwich, 1988–91.
Perimeter corridor, view
of both buildings from the
water site plan.

[70] Foster won this international competition in 1991; its other participants included S.O.M. and I.M. Pei, in addition to several German architects (such as ABB, Bofinger, HPP). Apartments and shops will occupy 100 000 square metres in a tower 185 metres high. Hanging gardens describe a spiral along the entire height and contribute to the tower's micro-climate.

This project's initial design suggests a much livelier version of the Hongkong Bank.[70] The projects for Frankfurt and Barcelona have very different programmes but nonetheless follow the same geometry: curved facets cluster around a stressed vertical axis. They possibly suggest a stylistic turning point for Sir Norman Foster and Partners.

By comparison, the crystalline purity of the built volume designed for the Microelectronics Park in Duisburg entirely follow the customary lines of Foster's work.

MICRO-ELECTRONICS PARK IN DUISBURG

The Duisburg project is located between the city centre and the university in Neudorf. A physical development plan was drawn up for regeneration of the quarter with the aim of replacing old, inefficient industrial buildings with new, more environmentally friendly ones. The plan provides for a new public park and three building complexes, of which the largest, the Micro Centre, comprises 12 blocks with a maximum height of five storeys. A boulevard divides them into two groups, with full-height, naturally glazed atriums in which public or semi-public activities can take place throughout the year. The climatic system will be regulated primarily by the passive energy released by the soil of the park.

The other two buildings are Foster's. They stand out by their distinctive forms: the Business Promotion Centre with its almond-shaped floor plan and a lightly vaulted roof sloping down over the longitudinal axis, and the Telematic Centre located near the roofs of the Micro Centre, a cylindrical volume with a slightly tilted roof.

Despite its idiosyncratic roof, the Telematic Centre represents a sober combination of the cylindrical Humana Tower and the Holiday Inn in The Hague. With its area of 3500 m^2, the Telematic Centre is the extension of an existing building. It is entered along a ramp that twists down and into the building, opening into a room designed for exhibitions and video presentations, beside which is a café. The building is dominated by a 12 m diameter central atrium. The centre provides the entire industrial park with the most modern telecommunications technology.

The Business Promotion Centre is eight storeys high with an area of 4000 m^2. A technical innovation here is the external cladding, which consists of three layers: a glass external skin, a cavity containing computer controlled blinds, and an inner layer consisting of transparent insulating material developed jointly with the client, Kaiser Bautechnik.

Interior of Duisberg
Business Promotion
Centre, top floor.

Section of the Telematic
Centre.

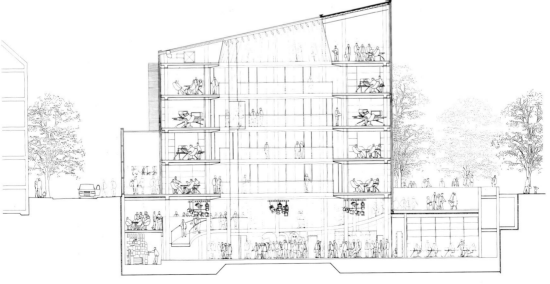

Interior of the Telematic
Centre, showing the
central atrium.

Commercial and residential building, Chelsea Reach, London, 1986–90. The lower floors contain the new offices of Foster Associates, access via the stairway (small photo).

All these prestigious projects, which were either completed or under construction or implementation at the beginning of the 1990s, should not allow three other less well-known works to be overlooked – works that demonstrate Foster's ability to vary his established repertoire in new and surprising ways without succumbing to random eclecticism. The commercial and residential building at Chelsea Reach in London, located on the Thames between Albert Bridge and Battersea Bridge, contains, among other institutions, the new offices of Foster Associates (now Sir Norman Foster and Partners). Structurally the building follows the classical division into a base, a middle section with apartments and a set-back roof with penthouse apartments; among them is the private apartment of the architect. Particularly impressive is the large studio (60 x 24 x 6.5 m), with a glazed longitudinal façade overlooking the Thames to the north, while all building services are combined in a block with a gallery on the south side. Even the access is spectacular: one reaches the reception via a roomy, four-flight top-lit staircase.[71] The entire office space has a suspended ceiling, and the team's most recent work is displayed on one of the large walls.

71 Very similar to the solution with the Médiathèque in Nîmes.

THE ITN BUILDING

While the architectural language of Chelsea Reach represents a refined version of that of the IBM building in Greenford, the building for the ITN television company on Gray's Inn Road in London and Century Tower for the Obunsha publishing group in Tokyo draw on other sources, from the repertoire of the Hongkong Bank. The London building, which is less spectacular than the one in Japan, can be understood as a kind of general synthesis. It combines the minimalism of Foster's early office buildings with his urban design-oriented work of the 1980s and his predilection for the large vertical atrium. The expressive force of the structure appears somewhat weakened here, however, and is essentially reduced to the architectural effect of the visible concrete, no doubt due to economic constraints. It has rightly been observed that this building demonstrates how an appropriate urban design form with a high quality interior can be achieved even under the financial constraints of a project financed by a development company. The building evolved through a collaboration between Independent Television News and the well-known developer Stuart Lipton of Stanhope Properties,[72] for whom Foster Associates had already built an office building in Stockley Park in 1987 and designed a three-storey office building in Chiswick, but with a square plan and diagonal atrium.

72 He became famous especially with his attempt to build a high-rise project by Mies van der Rohe in London, triggering a legal and journalistic battle between modernists and anti-modernists in the middle of the 1980s.

All these buildings have an atrium, which among its other functions supplies the lower storeys, including those in the basement, with natural light. As previously in the case of Willis Faber & Dumas, the

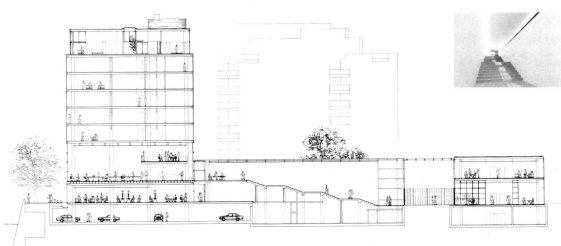

Headquarters of the ITN
television company,
London, 1988–90. View of
the atrium.
ITN. Frontage on Gray's
Inn Road.

atrium is the actual circulation space and like Stockley Park and Century Tower it also includes the bridges, which can present unusual, indeed dizzying spatial impressions and gives the interior of these commercial buildings a very distinctive character. The atrium combines amenity with technology, for it is a visible expression of the desire to create a bio-climatic micro-climate by the use of passive energy, solar energy, thermal pumps, and a cleverly designed climate-control system. To this end the ITN building employed the older method of extracting exhaust air between the glass outer walls of the building. The extract grills, incidentally, are visible on the façade.

The building not only takes account of its surroundings, but also respects them, which is not often the case in profit-oriented projects of this type. The upper floors are set back to minimize the bulk of the street elevation. Especially successful is the treatment of the transition to the pavement and street: the two lower floors are cut back behind a row of structural columns so that the neighbouring building on the other side of the narrow side street remains visible.

Century Tower was the first commission for Foster Associates in Japan. While the American market seemed to have been closed to him, several Japanese companies have turned to Foster with various projects. The 'tower of the century' was designed and built between 1988 and 1991 for the Obunsha publishing group. Though it recalls the tower of the Hongkong Bank, it responds to a very different cultural and urban situation.

The building is located on a major road in the northern district of Tokyo, near a busy railway line, but also near a historic neighbourhood with traditional low-rise buildings. A building with character and a certain elegance was required, thus making a break with the rest of the commercial architecture of Tokyo, which is 'without format and as bland as in many cities of the world' (Norman Foster).

Century Tower consists of two towers of 19 and 21 storeys, connected by a spectacular narrow atrium crossed by walkways. Double-height floor units alternate with mezzanines. This double-storey principle of organization, clearly expressed on the façades, gives the tower its special scale and distinctive appearance and recalls in formal terms the large column halls and scaffold buildings of old Japan. The very expressive structure contributes to the symbolic image of the building and at the same time liberates the office floors from obstruction by structural elements. Naturally the structure was also engineered to withstand the typhoons which regularly strike the country.[73]

[73] In contrast, seismic risks did not have to be taken into account in the case of the Hongkong Bank.

The ground floor contains a restaurant, an art gallery and a health club with a swimming pool beneath a glass roof whose curve was inspired by the silhouettes of ancient Japanese temples. The interior lighting also owes much to traditional Japanese architecture, to which Foster has been happy to refer ever since his first visit to Japan during the design of the Hongkong Bank. On the roof of the higher tower are a penthouse apartment and gallery spaces for the client; in its floor plan, which is based on diagonally bisected rectangles, it is related to the scheme of Foster's own apartment on Chelsea Reach. Century Tower possesses a certain grace and the sobriety and dynamism of the design, its spatial organization and the refinement of the details make the building an exceptionally successful creation of Foster Associates.

Century Tower, Tokyo,
1987–91. Drawing of the
complex with fitness
centre, overall view.

Century Tower. View up
into the atrium with the
connecting bridges.

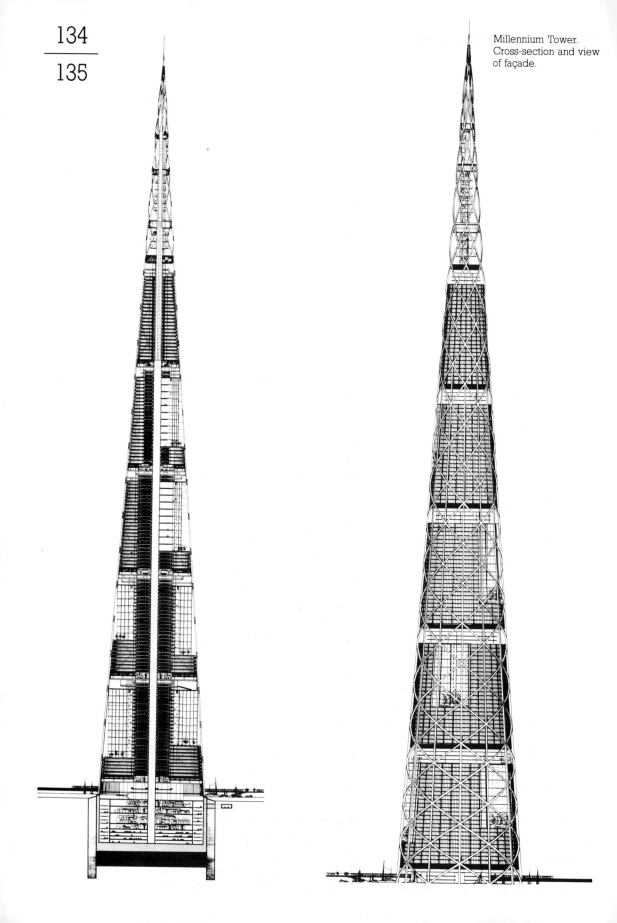

Millennium Tower.
Cross-section and view
of façade.

Millennium Tower

Of all the projects in which Foster Associates participated at the beginning of the 1990s, Millennium Tower is the most spectacular. At first glance it appears as Foster's entry in the competition for the highest building in the world, and in fact it could beat its rivals by several lengths: if this tower of the century were to be built, its 840 m would make it twice as high as the Sears Tower. Yet the project is equally a part of current international progress; it symbolizes Japan's response to the challenges of today; and, not least, it attempts to offer a solution to the problem of the city of today. On this subject the architect writes: 'Every decade has its turmoil, but it seems the 1990s will be particularly tumultuous. This, the last decade of the twentieth century, promises in terms of international perceptions to totally overturn assumptions which have been unquestioned for a generation and more. The inevitability of radical change in fundamental geopolitical alignments is already apparent. These changes, where only recently immutable truths seemed established, have occurred so rapidly, nothing now can be considered absolute. Comprehension of super power politics, military resourcing, economic systems, racism, consumerism to name a few, has become so volatile as to make any preconceptions questionable.

Nations, ethnic groups, minorities must be encouraged to a more harmonious existence on the planet. Responsible leadership must be demonstrated on issues such as environmental pollution, resources depletion, over population, urban blight. A role model must be developed for sensitive worldly response to the complex needs of human occupation. Japan, which now dominates the economic locomotion of this changing world, must widen the role to embrace the moralistic, humane ethic which needs to evolve in parallel with these cataclysmic developments. Economic power must be used to influence a more enlightened political/social agenda.'

The central theme of Millennium Tower is its urban character. The Japanese·company Ohbayashi commissioned Foster to prepare a study of the possibilities and effects of an architectural complex that would stand in isolation in the sea, in Tokyo Bay, and which would display a self-contained urban texture, a genuine city with 50 000 inhabitants on an area of roughly 1 000 000 m². In the mixture of its uses it will be comparable to New York's Fifth Avenue, Tokyo's Ginza or the Champs-Elysée in Paris. Foster's plans show once again that, even in the case of a megastructure such as this, he is more interested in the question of its use by people than in the technological challenge it represents, particularly since the structural technologies for building high-rise towers on difficult terrain are essentially already available. Here the architect sees new possibilities for urban development:

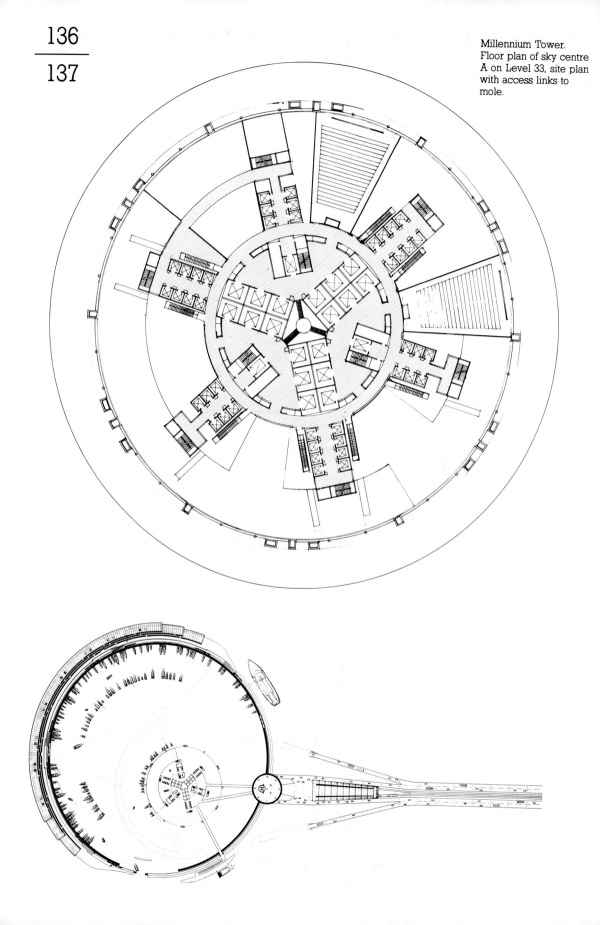

Millennium Tower.
Floor plan of sky centre
A on Level 33, site plan
with access links to
mole.

Millennium Tower.
Model – overall view
and view of the base of
the tower in the mole.

'The planner's preoccupation with strict zoning of human activity has been perhaps the single most destructive social evil of contemporary urbanism. As we have evolved from working with our hands to working with our minds, the twentieth century office building has replaced the nineteenth century factory as the central villain of alienation and dehumanization. The opportunity exists to return to a multifunctional existence, embracing endeavour and leisure, work and play, the making and spending of money, in a much richer diverse experience.'

At first sight the tower is impressive. It recalls two forms that stand for the technical achievements of our century: its slim shape evokes the rocket, while the complexity of its structure echoes the radio telescope. For Foster's architecture the result is an unusual visual punctuation: all his towers are topped by an antenna or some other element that emphasizes the summit, but Millennium Tower is itself a tip, a purely conical body whose top reaches into the sky like a glittering metal needle, accentuated by a laser beam. Drawing closer, one recognizes the 'sinews' of the helical external structure, which resembles that of the Humana Tower in Louisville. Yet while that building's cylindrical body is wrapped in a network of regular lozenges, the same principle, applied to the cone, leads to a horizontal elongation of the lozenges towards the base and a vertical elongation towards the top, this dynamic pattern emphasizing the conical form. The overall form, however, is neither purely expressive nor even aggressive, and its plasticity is not confined to the skyward-pointing gesture. Instead, on closer examination, the building reveals a distinctly human scale which overrides the image of the purely geometrical object.

The tower is designed in the proportions of one to seven. The top two sevenths, open and appearing almost empty from afar, are designated for viewing platforms, restaurants, antennae and collectors for wind and solar energy. The main section of the tower, divided into five zones of equal height, contains living accommodation in its upper section, offices in the lower. Access is provided according to the principle worked out for the Hongkong Bank: rapid access to the major zones and slower local connections, provided here by lifts. They are located in the supply core of the tower, which appears here for the first time in Foster's architecture, representing to a certain degree a return to the classical concept of a high-rise building.

Various structural forms were explored for increased wind resistance and earthquake security: prisms, groups of prisms, the cylindrical and finally the conical shape. The latter proved especially favourable from the point of view of construction costs, especially those of the foundations, and for construction time. For the purposes of construction, comprehensive studies led to the proposal of a moving service installation which is suspended on the building's structure and provides protection against bad weather. A building that carries its construction site along with it – what a picture for our time.

The intermediate spaces accessed by the lifts are also designed on the principle of the Hongkong Bank. Corresponding with the inhabited volumes they each serve, they each occupy five storeys and are effectively city centres, here known as 'sky centres'.[74] Each centre has special tasks and its own character. These are semi-public areas with terraces, hotels, restaurants, sports centres and shopping facilities, while the first six storeys, even more comprehensively equipped, form the public square of the city-building. To the south of this huge entrance hall lies a plaza open to the water.

Thanks to its multifunctionality, the spaces of the tower are to be active around the clock. Moreover, the tower is by no means an insulated, isolated world and the heterogeneous spaces are visible from the outside because of their transparent cladding, dispelling any notions of a 'lonely island'. A marina encircles the base of the tower, creating a visual transition between the verticality of the building and the horizontal expanse of the ocean; the visitor arriving by car, train or boat is surprised by the sudden change in character of the natural surroundings. Recreation areas and promenades created here will lure visitors from the mainland and create opportunities for interaction. The tower stands formally unfettered and without an axial reference inside this mole, whose circular plan forms resemble the workings of a watch; just as the tower itself evokes Frank Lloyd Wright's utopian project for a 'Mile-High Illinois Sky-City', its positioning recalls his Greater Baghdad project of 1957, with its autonomous, circular zones connected with the city by a large street axis.

Norman Foster is turning away from the traditional city with its advantages and disadvantages, but in contrast to the American architects he places great stress on preserving the density and activity of the old cities. One senses his enjoyment of the idea of living in a completely constructed environment, but it is also apparent that this is not a Utopian at work, he is not someone who wants to design an object solely for the appeal of its aesthetic form. Foster shows himself here as an architect who is almost equally a researcher, imbued with a positive vision of the modern world, and at the same time aware of the problems of its environment. So we may sum up the tower project and other Foster works in a single image, the image of a cocoon that allows the heavy caterpillar to transform into a butterfly, into something light, a cocoon permeated by light that will give birth to a different, new existence.

[74] "Here the residents will find places of identity comparable to the traditional square of an urban quarter where people meet and relax" (Norman Foster).

Principal projects

1994
Competition for British Museum Redevelopment, London, UK.*
Competition for Cardiff Bay Opera House, UK.
New offices at Holborn Circus, London, UK.
Competition for bridge at Millau, France.
Competition for Grande Stade, St Denis, Paris, France.
Competition for Centre de la Mémoire, Oradour sur Glanes, France.
Competition for Casino-Kursaal Oostende, Belgium.
Competition for Bangkok Airport, Thailand.
Zhongshan Guangzhou, 80 storey retail and office development, China.*
Al Faisaliah Complex, Riyadh, Saudi Arabia.*
Sea Life Centre, Birmingham, UK.
Sea Life Centre, Blankenberge, Belgium.

1993
New office and railway development, Kuala Lumpur, Malaysia.
Forth Valley Community Care Village, UK.
Headquarters for ARAG, Düsseldorf, Germany.
Masterplan for Lisbon Expo, Portugal.*
Masterplan for Corfu, Greece.
Competition for Hong Kong Convention and Exhibition Centre, Hong Kong.
London School of Economics Library, London, UK.
Offices for EDF (Electricité de France), Bordeaux, France.
Tennis Centre, Manchester, UK.
Headquarters for Timex, Connecticut, USA.
Street lighting for Decaux, Paris, France.
MTR platform edge screens, Hong Kong.
MTR signage system, Hong Kong.
MTR station furniture and components, Hong Kong.
MTR terminal, Hong Kong.
Wind turbine energy generator.
HACTL cargo building for new airport, Chek Lap Kok, Hong Kong.
Kowloon Canton Railway Station/Terminal Hong Kong.
South Kensington Millennium Project, London, UK.
Competition for National Gallery of Scottish Art, Glasgow, UK.
Design for Oresund Bridge, Copenhagen, Denmark.
Imperial War Museum, Hartlepool, UK.*
Competition for Exhibition Halls, Villepinte, Paris, France.

Competition for Urban Design at Porte Maillot, Paris, France.
Competition for Medieval Centre for Chartres, France.
Masterplanning Studies for Gare d'Austerlitz, Paris, France.
New Headquarters for Credit du Nord, Paris, France.

1992–
New airport at Chek Lap Kok, Hong Kong.*

1992–94
Extension to Joslyn Arts Museum, Omaha, Nebraska, USA.*
School of Physiotherapy, Southampton, UK.
House at Ludenscheid, Germany.

1992–93
Refurbishment and addition to the Hamlyn House, Chelsea, London, UK.
Marine simulator, Rotterdam, The Netherlands.
Clore Theatre, Imperial College, London, UK.

1992
Competition for New York Police Academy, New York, USA.
Congress Centre, Valencia, Spain.
Headquarters factory and warehouse for Tecno, Valencia, Spain.
Competition for Reichstag new German Parliament, Berlin, Germany.*
Offices, Tower Place, City of London, UK.
Yokohama Masterplan, Japan.
Competition for Business Park, Berlin, Germany.*
Manchester Olympic Bid Masterplan, UK.*
Competition for Spandau Bridge, Berlin, Germany.
Thames Valley Business Park, UK.
Station Poterie, Rennes, France.
High bay warehouse, Ludenscheid, Germany.
Masterplan for Ludenscheid, Germany.
Competition for Houston Museum of Fine Arts, USA.
Masterplan for Rotterdam, the Netherlands.
Masterplan for Imperial College, London, UK.
Competition for World Trade Centre, Berlin, Germany.
Shops and franchises for Cacharel, France.
Musée de la Préhistoire, Gorges du Verdon, France.*

1991–
New headquarters for Commerzbank, Frankfurt, Germany.*
Viaduct for Rennes, France.*

1991–93
Lycée Polyvalent Régional (Secondary School), Fréjus, France.*
New headquarters for Obunsha Corp., Yarai Cho, Tokyo, Japan.

1991–92
Cladding system for Jansen Vegla Glass.

1991
Kawana Houses, Japan.
Masterplan for Greenwich, London, UK.
Masterplan for Duisburg Harbour, Germany.*
Paint Factory, Frankfurt Colloquium, Frankfurt, Germany.*
Gateway office building to Spitalfields Redevelopment, London, UK.
Napp Laboratories, Cambridge, UK.
University of Cambridge Institute of Criminology, Cambridge, UK.
Office building for Stanhope Properties and County Natwest, London, UK.
New headquarters and retail building for Sanei Corp., Makuhari, Japan.
New headquarters for Agiplan, Mulheim, Germany.
Imperial War Museum Exhibition Hanger, Duxford, UK.
Canary Wharf Station for the Jubilee underground extension, London, UK.*

1990–95
Law Faculty of Cambridge University, Cambridge, UK.*

1990–93
House for M. Bousquet, Corsica, France.
Motoryacht for Japanese client.

1990
Masterplan for Berlin, Germany.
Masterplan for Cannes, France.
Masterplan for Nîmes, France.
Office building for Fonta, Toulouse, France.
Refurbishment of Brittanic House, City of London, UK.
Competition for Hotel du Département, Marseilles, France.
Competition for Congress hall, San Sebastian, Spain.
Competition for Fair Trade Centre, Berlin, Germany.

1989–92
New library for Cranfield Institute of Technology, UK.*

1989–91
Offices for Stanhope Properties, Chiswick Park Development, London, UK.
Street furniture for Decaux, Paris, France.
British Rail station, Stansted Airport, Stansted, UK.

1989
Passenger concourse building for British Rail, King's Cross, London, UK.
Millennium Tower, Japan.
Design Centre Essen, Germany.
Planning studies for the City of Cambridge, UK.
Office building DS2 at Canary Wharf, London.*
Apartments and offices, New York, USA.
Competition for Terminal 5, Heathrow Airport, London, UK.
Technology centres, Edinburgh and Glasgow, UK.
Office building for Jacob's Island Co., Docklands, London, UK.

1988–
Micro Centre, Duisburg, Germany.

1988–95
Underground railway system, Bilbao, Spain.*

1988–93
Business Promotion Centre and Telematic Centre, Duisburg, Germany.

1988–92
Telecommunications Tower, Torre de Collserola, Barcelona, Spain.*

1988–91
Crescent Wing at the Sainsbury Centre for Visual Arts, UEA, Norwich, UK.

1988–90
ITN new headquarters, Grays Inn Road, London, UK.

1988
Sackler Galleries, Jerusalem, Israel.
City of London Heliport, UK.
Shop for Esprit, Sloane Street, London, UK.
Contract carpet and tile design for Vorwerk.
Competition for Kansai Airport, Japan.
Pont D'Austerlitz, bridge across the river Seine, Paris, France.

Offices for Stanhope Securities, London Wall, City of London, UK.
Holiday Inn, The Hague, The Netherlands.

1987–92
Kawana House, Japan.

1987–91
Century Tower office building, Bunkyo-ku, Tokyo, Japan.

1987–89
Riverside housing and light industrial complex, Hammersmith, London, UK.
Offices for Stanhope Securities, Stockley Park, Uxbridge, UK.

1987
Hotel and club, Knightsbridge, London, UK.
Redevelopment masterplan, Kings Cross, London, UK.*
Competition for Turin Airport, Italy.
Hotel for La Fondiaria, Florence, Italy.
Shopping centre near Southampton for Savacentre, UK.
Bunka Radio Station, Yarai Cho, Tokyo, Japan.
Competition for Paternoster Square redevelopments, London, UK.

1986–90
Thameside Development – residential apartments and new offices for Foster Associates, Hester Road, London, UK.

1986
Salle de Spectacles, Nancy, France.
Headquarters for Televisa, Mexico City, Mexico.
Shop for Katherine Hamnett.
New York Marina, USA.

1985–91
New gallery complex, The Sackler Galleries, Royal Academy of Arts, Piccadilly, London, UK.

1985–87
Furniture system for Tecno, Milan, Spain.

1985
New offices for IBM, Greenford, UK.

1984–93
Centre d'Art Contemporian et Médiathèque, Carré d'Art, Nîmes, France.*

1984–86
IBM head office, major refit, Cosham, UK.

1982–85
New Radio Centre for BBC, London, UK.*

1982
Autonomous Dwelling (with Buckminster Fuller), USA.

1981–91
Third London Airport Stansted, UK:
    new terminal building
    new airside satellites
    landside airside coach stations
    terminal zone masterplan

1981–86
National Indoor Athletics Stadium, Frankfurt, Germany.*

1981
Foster Associates office, Great Portland Street, London, UK.
Competition for Billingsgate Fish Market, London, UK.

1980–83
Parts Distribution Centre for Renault UK limited, Swindon, UK.

1980
Planning studies for Statue Square, Hong Kong.
Students' Union Building, University College, London, UK.

1979–86
New headquarters for the Hongkong and Shanghai Banking Corporation, Hong Kong.*

1979
Granada Entertainment Centre, Milton Keynes, UK.
Shop for 'Joseph', Knightsbridge, London, UK.

1978–79
Foster Residence, Hampstead, London, UK.

1978
London Gliding Club, Dunstable Downs, UK.
Proposals for International Energy Expo, Knoxville, USA.
Open House Community Project, New York, USA.
Whitney Museum Development Project, New York, USA.

Further reading

1977–79
Technical Park for IBM, Greenford, UK.
Transportation interchange for LTE, Hammersmith, London, UK.

1976–77
Masterplan for St Helier Harbour, Jersey.

1975–76
Regional Planning Studies for Island of Gomera, Canaries.

1975
Fred Olsen Gate Redevelopment, Oslo, Norway.

1974–78
Sainsbury Centre for Visual Arts, UEA, Norwich, UK.

1974–75
Palmerston Special School, Liverpool, UK.

1974
Country club and marina, Son, Norway.
Travel agency for Fred Olsen Limited, Vestby, Norway.

1973–77
Aluminium extrusion plant for SAPA, Tibshelf, UK.

1973–75
Low Rise Housing, Bean Hill, Milton Keynes Development Corporation, UK.

1973–74
Headquarters for VW Audi NUS and Mercedes Benz, Milton Keynes, UK.

1972–73
Orange Hand Boys Wear Shops for Burton Group, UK.
Modern Art Glass Limited, Thamesmead, UK.

1971–75
Willis Faber & Dumas Head Office, Greyfriars, Ipswich, UK.

1971–73
Special Care Unit, Hackney, London, UK.

1971–72
Retail & Leisure Studies, Liverpool, Exeter and Badhoevedorp.

1971
Foster Associates Studio, London, UK.
Theatre for St. Peter's College, Oxford, UK.
Climatroffice.

1970–71
Fred Olsen Limited Passenger Terminal, Millwall, UK.
Computer Technology Limited, Hemel Hempstead, UK.
IBM Advance Head Office, Cosham, UK.

1970
Air-Supported Structure for Computer Technology Limited, Hertfordshire, UK.

1969
Factory Systems Studies.
Masterplan for Fred Olsen Limited, Millwall Docks, London, UK.

1968–69
Fred Olsen Limited Amenity Centre, Millwall, London, UK.

1967
Newport School Competition, UK.

1965–66
Reliance Controls Limited, Swindon, UK.

1965
Housing for Wates, Coulsden, UK.

1964–66
Skybreak House, Radlett, Hertfordshire, UK.
Creak Vean House, Feock, Cornwall, UK.

1964
Forest Road Extension, East Horsley, UK.
Mews Houses, Murray Mews, Camden Town, London, UK.
Cockpit, Cornwall, UK.

* Denotes winner of national or international competition.

The work of the architect is appearing in four volumes, edited by Ian Lambot. Volumes 1–3 are available from Watermark Publications or Ernst & Sohn:
Vol. 1, *Team Four & Foster Associates, Buildings and Projects 1964–1973, 1991.*
Vol. 2, *Foster Associates, Buildings and Projects 1971–1978, 1990.*
Vol. 3, *Foster Associates, Buildings and Projects 1978–1985, 1990.*

In German:
François Chaslin, Frédérique Hervet, Armelle Lavalou, *Norman Foster, Beispielhafte Bauten eines Spätmodernen Architekten*, Stuttgart: DVA, 1987 (French edition 1986).
Aldo Benedetti, *Norman Foster*, Zürich und München: Verlag für Architektur Artemis, 1990 (Italian edition 1988).
Colin Davis, *High-Tech Architektur*, pp. 56–58, Stuttgart: Hatje, 1988.

Collections:
Deyan Sudjic: *Norman Foster, Richard Rogers, James Stirling*. London: Thames and Hudson, 1986.
Architecture d'Aujourd'hui, NF 243, 1986 ('Projets, Réalisations 1980–1986').
Architecture + Urbanism, Special edition 1988.
Architectural Review, No. 1131, 1991 (Stansted Airport).

Hongkong Bank:
Process Architecture, Special issue No. 70, 1986.
Architectural Review, Special issue No. 1070, 1986.
Stephanie Williams, *Hongkong Bank: The building of Norman Foster's Masterpiece*, London: Cape, 1989.
Ian Lambot, *The Headquarters of the Hongkong and Shanghai Bank*, Watermark 1986.

Norman Foster. Sketches, edited by Werner Blaser, Birkhäuser Verlag Basel, Boston, Berlin 1991.

Picture credits

Acknowledgements

Arcaid, Architectural Photography
Picture Library: 16b, 17b
John Donat: 20b, 30b, 34/35
Julius Shulman, Los Angeles: 6, 9
James Stirling: 11
Daniel Treiber: 23t and b, 31

With kind permission from the archives of
Foster Associates:
Cameracraft: 15
Richard Davies: 38t, 45, 49t, 51, 58t, 59, 91tr
and br, 92, 93, 95, 96, 98b, 105t, 110t, 112t,
115, 120, 125t and m, 126, 127, 137
Dennis Gilbert: 109, 116m and b, 121t, 122,
123
Birkin Haward: 42m
Helmut Jacoby: 98t
Ken Kirkwood: 36, 37b, 105b, 110tl, 111,
112b, 114
Ian Lambot: 55, 74, 75, 77, 85, 87, 106/107,
108, 110b, 112m, 131, 132, 133
Tim Street-Porter: 19t, 25, 27b, 30t

Additional photos and drawings were provided by the office of Foster Associates.

Cover:
Hongkong and Shanghai Bank, Atrium
(Photo: Jan Lambot).

Sir Norman Foster (Photo: Rudi Meisel).

Once again my very warm thanks to Sir
Norman Foster and Partners for their kind
support. Special thanks go to Sir Norman
Foster and Chris Seddon, Graham Phillips,
Ken Shuttleworth and Rodney Uren for
their explanations, as well as to Katy
Harris, Fiona Millar and Sarah Conrado for
their help in finding illustrations.

Thanks also to Ruth Marquès from the
French Ministère de l'Equipement et du
Logement, who allowed me to study one of
the most complex and advanced buildings
of our age, the Hongkong Bank, within the
framework of a research programme.

I would like to thank Marc N. Vigier and
François Chaslin, who facilitated visits to
many buildings of Sir Norman Foster, as
well as Branwen Treiber and Alan Levitt
for their help on these occasions as well
as in establishing the first contacts with Sir
Norman Foster and Partners.

Finally I thank my research team, Guy
Rumé, Philippe Silvin, and Guillaume
Danchin, for their work on this book, as
well as Hélène Treiber for her help and
her encouragement.

Index